AN INTRODUCTION TO KARATE

AN INTRODUCTION TO KARATE

KEN SINGLETON

ILLUSTRATED BY JULIAN SMITH

An OPTIMA book

© Ken Singleton 1989

First published in 1989 by
Macdonald Optima, a division of
Macdonald & Co. (Publishers) Ltd

A member of Maxwell Pergamon Publishing Corporation plc

British Library Cataloguing in Publication Data

Singleton, Ken
    An introduction to karate. – (Martial arts series)
    1. Karate – Manuals
    I. Title   II. Series
    796.8'153

    ISBN 0-356-17219-8

Macdonald & Co. (Publishers) Ltd
66-73 Shoe Lane
Holborn
London
EC4P 4AB

Typeset in Century Schoolbook
by Leaper & Gard Ltd, Bristol, England

Printed and bound in Great Britain by
The Guernsey Press Co. Ltd., Guernsey, Channel Islands.

DEDICATION

For my Father, who died not knowing what all the fuss
was about.

CONTENTS

PREFACE

This book aims to take a sober look at a subject which, in the West, often gets a bad press. Karate is too often associated with defeated opponents, calloused hands and broken roof tiles. At best it is shown to satisfy the West's need to compete and win, as though it were a kind of martial sport attracting accolades and prizes for the mantelpiece; at worst as an effective way to sharpen aggressive instincts by direct physical means and, by so doing, to whet the appetite for conflict. The assumption is that Westerners can only come to grips with the martial arts if they are described as either physical or competitive, or both, and that any spiritual practices, while being fully compatible with Eastern inscrutability, are almost totally alien to Western temperament. Westerners are felt to be unable to immerse themselves fully in systems for which those in the East are predestined.

A book which intends to cut through this tough, competitive image may not be so immediately sensational, but true karate is exciting enough and nothing is gained from fabrication. The task is to take the reader beyond the bar-room brawl and the tournament arena, where all the struttings and gesturings of sport are on display, and to place karate where it belongs, alongside the other martial and fine arts of the East, all of which have a common purpose. It is hoped in this way that its true character will shine through.

Karate, at least on the surface, is an understandable target for the approach which associates it with thuggishness and rivalry, as many of its attacking movements are specifically designed to do the greatest possible harm to another person in the shortest possible time. The crucial point, though, is that the other person exists only in one's mind, never in the flesh. So, as opponents are always imagined, the true target of all techniques is actually the person performing them. Students practise movements which appear to form a repertoire for the physical destruction of others, but which in fact aim to eliminate the wasting elements within the students themselves.

This has not always been the case; the historical roots of all the martial arts reveal systems of armed and unarmed combat borne out of the need to survive on the field of battle or to ward off hostile bandits in lonely mountain passes. The same potentially ruthless physical techniques remain to this day, albeit somewhat refined, but along the way fundamental principles of Zen have been adopted, causing all those who practise the martial arts to regard self-improvement as their ultimate objective.

What comes down to us today, then, is a synthesis of the practical and the spiritual, a combination of the body and the spirit. The balance must be preserved. Where there is an over-emphasis on the physical aspects of karate, students will achieve, at the very most, only a level of technical ability equivalent to high-scoring sportsmen. Equally, an over-zealous approach to the mental disciplines results in mere empty philosophizing if technical skill has been sacrificed. The point of departure of this book is the unity of the physical and the mental, which finds concrete expression in rigorous movement.

Ken Singleton

PART 1 INTRODUCTION AND HISTORY

Legend and historical probability, mostly undocumented, at best give us a cloudy understanding of the early origins of karate in China. These weaponless fighting systems, probably crude, unstructured, but effective, gradually penetrated into Okinawa and there blended with already established hand-to-hand fighting techniques. It is not until earlier this century, when Funakoshi Gichin visited Japan from Okinawa and fired Japanese enthusiasm, that the picture becomes clear and the basis was laid for modern Japanese-style karate.

CHINA

As far back as 5000 BC there is thought to have existed in India a system of weaponless fighting techniques, later to be known as *vajramushti*. It is thought that Bodhidharma, revered as the 28th patriarch in the Indian lineage following on from the Buddha and the first patriarch of Zen in China, was a member of the class in southern India which practised these techniques, so he could well have been familiar with them. (To this day images of Bodhidharma, the blue-eyed monk who became known for his imperturbable 'sitting' for nine years facing a wall, are still popular with children in the East in the form of lead-bellied, legless dolls, which insist on returning to the upright position however hard or regularly pushed.)

A popular Chinese legend tells how Bodhidharma travelled the long, treacherous journey overland from India to China sometime after AD 520, to instruct Emperor Wu of the Liang dynasty in the tenets of Zen Buddhism. That he survived this remarkable journey, thousands of miles of hostile, uncharted terrain, plagued by marauding bandits, is seen as proof of his extraordinary strength and further suggests some degree of self-defence ability. Having failed on his arrival in China to gain favour with Emperor Wu, he settled at the Shaolin monastery in Honan province, guiding the student monks in their search for true enlightenment. However, his training methods were so rigorous that the monks regularly collapsed through sheer exhaustion. Explaining that Buddhism aims at nothing less than the salvation of the soul, and that the body and soul, being inseparable, need to be equally strong, he taught the monks a system of physical and mental exercises embodied in the *I-chin* sutra as a way of developing in them the rigid disciplines required. As time passed, and the monks practised and studied Bodhidharma's methods, they gained the reputation of being China's most formidable exponents of what came to be called *Ch'uan Fa*, 'fist way', now known as Kung Fu.

During these first hesitant days of its development, karate (if we are justified at this stage to call it that) quite possibly fused in some ways with the existing Chinese fighting techniques, said to have become widely established up to 1000 years before this time (and even much earlier than this, if we are to believe reports that the armies of the Yellow Emperor, Huang Ti, practised a form of what became Kung Fu and not simply an arbitrary, undisciplined form of thuggery on the battlefield). In any case, Chinese monks, during the following centuries, became increasingly able to defend themselves against bandits and indiscriminate assassins who systematically set mountain ambushes during the monks' pilgrimages. It may seem odd that the violent tenor of life during these times should produce the makings of a self-defence discipline not from the warring factions, or even from those whose trade was vulgar, aggressive confrontation, but from religious groups concerned more with inner harmony and personal development than the rough and tumble of physical conflict.

The monks, without question, were physically well trained, disciplined and mentally secure, but as regards any hostile attitude towards their fellow men they were woefully under-motivated and ill-equipped. What quite likely made the difference between them and their tormentors in the mountains was that they trained their bodies not as instruments of aggression or even for self-protection or survival, but as a form of meditation and as a vital link in their search for self-knowledge. For they had absorbed much of Taoist thought into their everyday lives, developing an organic union of physical and mental practices. Physical ability was not viewed merely as an end in itself, but as a measure of their struggle to look inward at themselves. Taoism, founded in 600 BC by Lao Tzu, has had, and still has, a major influence on thought and culture in the East and on the martial arts as a whole. It continues today to be the main philosophical force behind all Eastern arts, although the Japanese do not immediately recognize Taoist influences on aspects of their culture, tending instead to put under the banner of Zen anything that might derive from Taoist roots.

What we see from the monks at this stage is an effective but probably still relatively unsystematic fighting system used for self-defence and based on a union of physical and mental strength. It is these Shaolin forms of weaponless techniques which over the centuries filtered into Okinawa.

OKINAWA

Okinawa is the main island of the Ryuku chain, a narrow band of islands scattered like stepping stones from Kyushu, the southernmost part of Japan, to Taiwan, in the East China Sea. (In 1971 Okinawa attracted the world's attention when Yokoi, a Japanese World War II soldier, was discovered, having lived in a hand-dug, underground cavern since 1945, still half believing there was a war to fight. For the Japanese, still reeling to some extent from the writer Yukio Mishima's fanatical demands for a return to traditional military values, Yokoi posed the problem of whether he should be honoured as a hero or ridiculed as a fool.)

There is good reason to believe that the Shaolin fighting techniques were gradually penetrating into Okinawa from the sixth and seventh centuries onwards, along with many other elements of Chinese culture. And by the fourteenth century a fighting system combining both Chinese and Okinawan methods was quite well developed through the regular exchange of missionaries, traders and students. This was further strengthened in the fifteenth century when China's civil envoys to Okinawa were replaced by a military delegation, many of whom were noted for their skill in a martial art known as Chinese kempo.

Over the next two centuries a ban on all weapons was twice imposed, which had the effect of unifying the hand-to-hand fighting systems and greatly increasing their rate of development. First, King Haishi of the Okinawan Sho dynasty united the Ryuku island into a single kingdom, confiscating all weapons in an attempt both to ensure law and order and to discourage political military rivals. Then, in 1609, Okinawa fell under the rule of the Satsuma clan of Kyushu, and for a second time all weapons were seized and banned. The result of this was an increase in resentment and antagonism on the part of the Okinawans towards their Japanese overlords and the consolidation, over the next few centuries, of a weaponless fighting system to be called Okinawa-te.

At the same time the Okinawan peasants began to adapt various farming implements for use as weapons — the rice flail (*nunchaku*), the threshing fork (*sai*), rice grinder handles (*tonfa*) and long and short staves (*bo* and *jo*). It is likely that the peasants' action was merely a form of defiance against the weapons ban. But for the untrained or underprivileged the tendency may be to reach for the nearest sharp tool or blunt object when official forms of self protection are denied. However crude and inelegant these improvised weapons were, and for whatever reasons they were first employed, they were gradually raised to a higher status. Some chose to refine the use of these weapons into independent artistic systems, still studied in the East today; incorporated with karate movements the results can be uniquely expressive forms, equal in grace, precision and dynamic lines of the body to any gymnastic floor exercise. Applied in more general terms, Oriental dancers, jugglers and acrobats still reveal the source of their performances to have originated from the development of these basic farming implements of the peasants. Those studying karate, who were usually from the more privileged or *samurai* classes, experimented with these weapons, not as a serious alternative to karate but to gain new perspectives and because in feudal times warriors had been encouraged to become proficient in a wide variety of weapons and fighting systems.

Officials from Satsuma were frequently to be found on the islands during the years of prohibition, checking that the ban was strictly observed. Karate thrived, though, at least among a privileged and determined few, out of sight behind closed doors. Where it was visible was in the expansive movements of folk dance; rather than the graceful elegance employed in folk dances of the other Japanese islands, Okinawan dancers used expressive and vigorous arm and leg movements, not unlike many used in the karate of the time.

The second ban on weapons persisted into the years of Meiji (1868-1912, the period of the reign of Emperor Meiji), partly because the ancient decree lingered on in the minds of the people. Okinawa-te, or karate (Chinese hand), as it became known, remained underground, and although it was only practised clandestinely, it gained in popularity until it finally regained official recognition from the Japanese Ministry of Education in the early years of this century and became part of the school curriculum.

The man responsible for introducing karate into Japan, Funakoshi Gichin, was born in Shuri, Okinawa, in 1868, significantly the first year of the Meiji Restoration, when the Emperor was reinstated to his office, which, since the Kamakura era (1185-1333) had been administered by the Shoguns, the military generals. At that time Japan was virtually forced by the USA to open its doors to the West, and the Meiji government, in the broad and sweeping programme of reforms which followed, attempted to bring itself in line with Western ideas, even to the extent of jettisoning deeply-rooted traditions dear to the Japanese character. A total ban on all traditional forms of martial arts was proposed, such as judo (the gentle Way), kendo (the Way of the sword), kyudo (the Way of the bow) and karate, as these seemed to belong too much to the past to have a place in future plans. The warrior class, the main pillar of society up to the end of the Tokugawa period (1600-1868), was dissolved, the *samurai* being raised to the level of nobility or absorbed into the middle classes. In 1871 the *samurai* found themselves in the invidious position of being liable, like all male citizens, no matter from what rank or class, to compulsory military service, and in 1876 they were even forbidden to carry swords.

It was under these conditions that Funakoshi Gichin spent his early days in Okinawa. A sickly child and a frail boy, he was not expected to live a long life. It was suggested to him at the age of 11 that the study of karate might improve him physically. And from this time until his death at the age of 88 he devoted his life to the study and development of karate in Okinawa and Japan — giving shape and structure to ill-defined techniques, introducing progressive systems of training, redefining and simplifying names and, perhaps most importantly, protecting the delicate balance of the body and mind from the rush of an uncaring century.

JAPAN

Although this book is principally concerned with Japanese karate, specifically the style called Shotokan, it should not be assumed that karate developed relentlessly over the centuries in other Eastern countries and is now exclusive to Japan. Karate in various forms, as well as many other weaponless fighting techniques, still thrives in most of the Orient, although even today much is only vaguely represented in Britain.

To Western eyes Japan has shown itself in many ways to be expert in taking up ideas from outside and developing them independently into typical Japanese arts. Rarely is anything taken up in its entirety though: instead the Japanese approach is to select what is thought useful in practical terms and to ditch whatever is thought inappropriate to the Japanese context.

Karate, with its essential ingredients that we have today, was not introduced into Japan until earlier this century. But so completely has it been absorbed that it now displays all the signs of being entirely of Japanese origin. The rapidity of its absorption is not surprising, so naturally does it sit beside the principles and aims of the other arts, all once infused with the spirit of Chinese Taoism and Zen, and all at various times taken up and embraced by the Japanese. Archery (*kyudo*), the art of swordsmanship (*kendo*), the Way of tea (*chado*), the Way of writing (*shodo*), the Way of flowers (*kado*), and so on, originated not in Japan but in China, and even judo, officially created in Japan, has its spiritual roots in Chinese Taoism.

Karate can thus be seen to be in perfect harmony with these other martial and fine arts, whose practical aspects now principally serve a meditative purpose. The paradox is how the non-violent philosophical movements of Taoism and Zen were so enthusiastically embraced by a social class whose day-to-day trade was homicide. But when the emphasis on actually slaying opponents became of less importance in the Japanese tradition of martial arts the ways of combat reverted to what they had always been in China — a way to self-knowledge. The principal aims of archery and swordsmanship are now not to hit a target or neatly cut an opponent in two; the aims of the tea ceremony and flower arranging are not only concerned with taste or aesthetics. Equally, karate aims not to produce healthy street fighters or competition winners, but to promote the confrontation with ourselves.

Funakoshi Gichin

Funakoshi Gichin went to Japan in 1922 to give a number of talks and demonstrations under the auspices of the Ministry of Education. Karate at this time was little known on mainland Japan, so what his audiences saw was relatively new to them, although other martial arts, judo and kendo in particular, were studied compulsorily in the high schools. This new martial art so impressed the Japanese that Funakoshi Gichin was persuaded to stay and spread its popularity. Previously a school teacher, he remained in Japan doing odd jobs to subsidize his temporary *dojo* (training hall, literally 'place of the Way').

Growth was rapid, particularly in the universities (which still remain the strongholds of the martial arts in Japan) and among political figures and those favourably placed — doctors, lawyers, scholars, artists, etc. — to enhance the reputation of karate in the public eye when the new Shotokan *dojo* was opened to the general public in 1938.

Funakoshi Gichin's initial training method was centred around the teaching and repetition of *kata* — set formal movements involving blocks and counter attacks against a number of imaginary opponents (see page 114). but this was not felt to meet the needs of the younger generation, who were used to the combative nature of judo and kendo in the schools. As a result Funakoshi Gichin picked techniques from the *katas* and developed them into a variety of sparring movements practised with a partner: *Gohon kumite* (five-step sparring), *Kihon-ippon kumite* (basic one-step sparring), *Jyu-ippon kumite* (one-step free-sparring), *Jyu kumite* (free sparring) (see page 123). It was a difficult decision to make, as karate up to this point had been the practice and perfection of *kihon* (basics) and *kata*, performed repetitively and without a partner. But it was fundamentally to change the nature of karate and how it was to be regarded in the twentieth century. We are again confronted with a paradox. For the reputation of karate as a weaponless fighting system is founded on the idea that it is essentially a sparring system practised rigorously in pairs, yet sparring was not a part of karate until comparatively recently when it arrived in Japan from Okinawa.

It is perhaps fortunate for the development of karate in the West that these new sparring techniques were introduced, as they immediately offered the possibility for competition. Without this possibility it may be that karate would have remained a philosophical artistic form, albeit with a specific purpose, unknown or unexploited in the West, where there is often an almost obsessive need to measure achievement through competition.

These new sparring techniques were introduced in the early 1930s, and in 1936 the All Japan Collegiate Karate Union was formed and began to raise funds for a new permanent *dojo*, the first of its kind in Japan, which finally opened in 1938. This new *dojo* was called 'Shotokan', Funakoshi Gichin's pen name, which he used in his youth to sign his Chinese poems. The name that became attached to the largest and most successful karate 'style' thus has no great arcane significance; in Japanese *Shoto* simply means 'pine waves', while *kan* means 'building'. 'Shotokan-ryu', therefore, means 'the style they practise at Shoto's building'. In fact 'Shotokan' was called a 'style' against Funakoshi Gichin's wishes, by outsiders, those of his own students and those from the two other schools, Shito-ryu and Goju-ryu, who had broken away to form less significant styles of their own. Various of these styles — Shotokai, Wado-ryu and Kyokushinkai, for example — have gained footholds in Britain, and it is not impossible to find styles operating under impressive-sounding names all claiming excellence and far-reaching historical traditions.

The 1930s: a decade of change

In 1935, during a decade of major change in the structure of karate, Funakoshi Gichin's book *Karate-do Kyohan* was published. It was here that the very essence of what karate stood for was challenged.

Up to this time 'karate' had been written with characters from the Tang dynasty meaning 'Chinese hand' (*kara*, Chinese; *te*, hand). In *Karate-do Kyohan* Funakoshi Gichin proposed that the character for *kara* be changed to mean 'empty', more accurately reflecting the nature of karate as a Japanese art. The character he chose for *kara* was from the Buddhist tradition; also pronounced 'ku' it suggests 'rendering oneself empty' and has broad universal significance. To justify this change he wrote:

> As a mirror's polished surface reflects whatever stands before it and a quiet valley carries even small sounds, so must the student of karate render his mind empty of selfishness and wickedness in an effort to react appropriately toward anything he might encounter. This is the meaning of *kara*, or 'empty', of karate.

This change of the written characters may appear to the Westerner a mere inconsequential trifling with words, but among the traditional Okinawan masters, who thought it was wrenching karate away from its Okinawan and Chinese roots, it caused a tremendous uproar, and more than two years of haggling passed before it was accepted.

A more fundamental change outlined in *Karate-do Kyohan* went deep to the very nature and purpose of karate as a martial art. This was not simply a revision of wording, but involved the movement from karate-jutsu to karate-do, from the technique of karate for practical purposes, that is the best and surest way to kill, to its specialization based on the path of man toward self-knowledge. Karate-jutsu fitted in to the wider field of bujutsu, which embraced the technical disciplines of all the martial arts, and which, in the pre-Tokugawa period (1600-1868) encouraged warriors to establish themselves in a wide variety of weapons. Based solely on practical considerations, the wide-ranging use of weapons was designed for those constantly fighting for their lives on the field of battle, and had no other intention than to increase their chances of victory. During Tokugawa the arts were separated into distinct skills — swordsmanship, archery, spearmanship, etc. — each one being practised exclusively. Bujutsu, the broad use of the martial arts as instruments of murder, had become budo, the Way to self-improvement (*do*, Way or path) through the intensive practice of a single chosen discipline.

What Funakoshi Gichin proposed was that, just as bujutsu had become budo, karate-jutsu should become karate-do ('empty-hand Way'). The emphasis should be directed away from conflict and towards man himself. What is more, karate should be studied as an independent discipline, not as part of a package of martial art skills, including other forms and weapons only if they gave depth to the understanding of karate. For the Japanese believe that the serious study of more than one martial art, particularly in the early stages, pulls the spirit in more than one direction.

The popularity of Funakoshi Gichin's new *dojo* during the latter years of the 1930s made it necessary for a system of grades to be introduced. These still exist today:

kyu grades for the nine coloured belts (which get
progressively darker as rank increases); and thereafter
dan grades for black belts (see page 92).

A further change during this time was Funakoshi
Gichin's new design of the karate uniform (*gi*). Before this
time, in Okinawa, all students wore a version of the
traditional kimono, called a *hakama*. These are divided
into legs and give the impression of a wide skirt, of heavy
cloth and dark blue in colour. (The *hakama* is still worn in
Japan today in other martial arts such as kendo and
archery). There was still a rigid class system operating in
Japan at the time, reflected in the different dress worn by
separate levels of society. But the new karate *gi* was
designed to be worn by anyone, regardless of class or social
standing. The same design is still worn today; a
combination of the judo *gi* (although of thinner material)
and the *hakama*, and white in colour to symbolize purity of
intentions (see page 76).

The 1940s to the present

After the Second World War martial arts in Japan were
curtailed by the edict of the General Headquarters of
Allied Powers, until the ban was lifted in 1948. Karate,
however, avoided these measures, as it had among its
followers officials whose influence was used at the
Ministry of Education to claim that karate was, in fact, a
form of Chinese boxing, a sport, and therefore a harmless
pastime. Then in 1949 high-ranking followers of karate
organized themselves into the Japan Karate Association,
which in 1955 was officially incorporated as an
educational body under the Ministry of Education.

Masatoshi Nakayama, who was to replace Funakoshi
Gichin as Chief Instructor of the Japan Karate
Association upon Gichin's death in 1956, had for some time
been researching the possibility of introducing sport or
tournament karate. It was thought to be a necessary
addition to karate, to give it impetus abroad and a more
popular appeal in a modern competitive world. The main
concern was that competition might replace the strong

ideals of karate, based as they are on the repetition of rigorous basic techniques derived from the traditional *kata* (set forms). But little damage was done to the basic principles when the first All Japan Championships were held in 1957, although it is now becoming less easy to say that competitions take second place in the minds of many karate students.

PART 2
KARATE: SPORT OR ART?

KARATE AND WESTERN SPORT

It is quite natural to think that many activities of the East are still alien to Western man. Karate and the other martial arts may appear so thoroughly Eastern as to be impenetrable by even the most ardent Western enthusiast. This is not helped by the fact that it is almost impossible to think of a Western sport or physical activity which has aims even remotely resembling those of the martial arts. None, certainly, are designed specifically to improve self-protection through the practice of systematically planned movements, while at the same time developing the spiritual character of the performer. In fact, direct spiritual development is not one of the functions of Western sport and is certainly not one of the reasons for its popularity.

Few Western sports have an application which is fundamentally very far removed from the actual sporting purpose. That is, it is not the aim in the West to project the mental or physical benefits of sport from the playground, pitch or gym into the broader context of everyday life. When involved in sport our 'normal' lives are suspended. We try our best at whatever sport we do, try to accept success or failure gracefully, and return afterwards to our normal lives. Our sporting arenas are usually confined within physically limited areas set aside for the sole purpose of sport. While there we abide by rules set down to ensure that all concerned know the legal limits of the game or activity. When the whistle or hooter sounds the spell is broken and normal life is taken up again. It is true to say, of course, that it is hoped that by playing sport strength of character, self-discipline and a healthy respect for other people will result. But, in the West, these are more or less by-products, incidental to the main thrust of the activity, which is to try our best to win.

Western sport in itself rarely contains the ingredients to improve character; instead it is through such things as enduring miserable weather conditions, ignoring injuries bravely, recovering quickly from foul play, standing up to 'pressure'. Perhaps it is through sport that Western society expresses its interpretation of life and the world, but it is by means of extravagant displays, extreme gestures, big words, which have the effect of exciting some people and appalling others. But such sporting behaviour is regarded as normal, and is generally accepted, so long as it stops at the changing room door and does not spill over into everyday life.

Sport in the West has now reached such a level of gravity that to challenge its principles or even slightly doubt its benefits amounts almost to insolence. Sporting prowess has to a large extent become the measure of an individual's stature and even the general health of nations. From our first school sports day onwards we are encouraged to be unashamedly competitive. We learn quickly that most credit is to be gained from winning, some from coming a gallant second, and little but scorn from refusing to take part. Those who do well at sports usually have the most friends and are generally looked up to by others. We are given a 'house' and a colour, which usually remain etched on our memory for life. The names of 'houses' are those of scientists, scholars, inventors or major figures of literary or intrepid achievement. House members, then, have a lot to look up to. They also become responsible to a group and are expected to take this responsibility seriously, as the reputation of others depends on it. Any esteem and honour which we win will tend to accrue to the general benefit of the whole group.

It is assumed our best results will always be achieved through healthy competition, even to the point of thinking that all practice beforehand will merely be preparation for the 'real thing'. The will to win, fighting spirit and so on take precedence over good technique, so it matters little that we dash for the winning post or head for goal in complete technical disarray, so long as the adrenalin of competition is carrying us there.

These early introductions to sport are assumed to endure into adult life, so anything that hints of sport necessarily brings out the competitor in us and we look around for the opposition. As concerns such activities as karate and the other martial arts there is the tendency, at least in the early stages of training, to regard them as sport. That way we can more easily apply the principles and aims we are familiar with in the West, and what is obviously Eastern may, as a result, seem less alien.

Sport in the West follows an irrepressible logic. It involves winning, almost at any cost. Winning is a way of showing ourselves superior, the evidence of which tends to confer on us a semblance of superiority in general. What is at stake is often personal prestige. Winning presupposes an opponent. During competition it is best if the opponent puts up a strong enough fight to make us work hard, for that makes the feeling of tension and uncertainty worthwhile. The feeling of satisfaction we get from winning often mounts with the presence of spectators because we are then the centre of attention — they do not have to be close friends or members of our own team, outsiders are sufficient. The essence of the sporting image is to dare, to take risks, bear uncertainty and endure tension, all of which adds to the importance of the sport and, as they increase, enables the players or performers to forget it is only sport and believe it to be something serious with a serious purpose. The purpose in the West is to emerge victorious. There is little pretence that personal development or spiritual values are part of this. We stop short of actually cheating to achieve victory, as that spoils the game, although such terms as 'sportsmanship' and the 'professional foul' to some extent give the lie to our moral judgment in this respect. But we are quite prepared to allow a painstakingly developed technique to break down during fierce competition, as we feel it is this that often blocks the spirit to win. Most likely, though, it is this very egotistical desire to win or achieve that is itself the main obstacle to progress in sport, as well as in our normal everyday lives. The notion that we are more likely to win if we fiercely set our minds on it is very Western. For the Japanese, the more certain way of achieving good results is by wanting to play well, that is, by resisting any breakdown in technique or form, as when half our attention is on the finish it only leaves the other half to get us there. Apart from this, victory is hollow if the dignity of technique is completely sacrificed.

Gichin Funakoshi, in his short autobiography, *Karate-do: My Way of Life*, recalls watching an Okinawan tug of war:

The tug of war, a popular sport on the island, is often engaged in during one of our numerous festivals. Our tug of war is quite different from those practised in other prefectures. For one thing, it is a great deal more dynamic, as anyone who has witnessed an Okinawan tug of war will agree. And it is most definitely not a sport for children . . . What I learned from these tugs of war is that the team is intent only on winning will usually fail to do so, while the team that enters the contest in order to enjoy the sport without worrying too much about winning or losing will frequently emerge victorious. The observation holds as true for a karate bout as for a tug of war.

Wanting to win only strengthens the competitive spirit, which is based on, among other things, the urge to measure one's own achievement against others. The hierarchical structure of karate, with its system of gradings and belt colours, seems almost to invite or tempt students to compare themselves. But this assumes that belt colours are awarded merely for technical ability, whereas personal maturity, effort and inner substance have just as much to do with it, although they, of course, are not so obviously on show.

Technical ability alone is often the preserve of the natural athlete, and this often leads in the West to swaggering over-confidence and jostling admirers. For the antics of 'sportsmen' are tolerated in the West, even encouraged, as any audience loves to see signs that their heroes are indeed only human. Spectators, in fact, are usually far more sympathetically inclined towards competitors the more human weaknesses they display. Victory seems more touching when it comes their way. All shows of petulance, rebellion and so on are far more likely to strain the patience of the referee or umpire than outrage an audience, as they are thought to be signs of healthy individuality. It is only the spoil sport that is not tolerated, as he tends to break down the barriers of the magic sporting formula by failing to recognize any of its limits — quite simply he spoils the game. In the West, then, there exists no system to expel or banish over-confidence or conceit from a sportsman's make-up, so long as results are good. Indeed, moods and gestures may be encouraged in case results decline.

In the martial arts *dojo*, however, the story is very different. The essential characteristic is humility. Without this, contests, displays, challenges, struttings and preenings prevail, all factors of sport and 'play' which are a particular feature of animal behaviour.

There is a Japanese saying: 'When a nail sticks up, knock it down!' Pride and vanity must be mercilessly destroyed to allow a clear, untainted spirit freedom to emerge. Japanese methods of dealing with this are so unlike Western ways of thinking as to appear almost barbaric. In a Japanese *dojo* proud and vain students will be broken down ruthlessly with no apparent regard for their self-esteem or dignity. The ground has to be cleared, as though arrogance is the product of an evil spirit which has to be cast out. Juniors (*kohai*) who show signs of arrogance will be tormented by seniors (*sempai*) or teachers (*sensei*), who casually dismiss all spirit and technique as futile. The most perfect technique is thought to be worthless if coupled with a bad attitude. And so vain students are made to fight, and they will be unceremoniously dumped to the floor for much of the time. There is no antagonism involved, no bitterness. It is almost a ritualistic affair and both sides know its purpose. After 15 minutes the students do not think they can go on, but there is no let up, no rest, no breathing space. They continue for 30 minutes, for an hour, for a time they thought was well beyond them. They reach such extremes of exhaustion that when it stops they realize to what depths their levels of endurance and spirit will go. This may continue for weeks, or perhaps months, during which time there is no escape for the student: every scrap of vanity must be allowed to fall away.

It is not simply a question of knocking the student into shape or beating him into submission, for the Japanese firmly believe that beneath the surface of everyone lies a true nature, which such things as arrogance and over-confidence suppress. It is a matter, in the East, then, of freeing what is believed to be already present — man already *is* what he seeks. In the West, however, it is thought that ability, spirit and so on need to be taught, they are additions. This explains to some extent the vastly different attitudes towards teaching sport or any other physical activity. In the West it is wordy — the student is goaded, coerced, bullied, encouraged by a trainer or coach. Every technical detail is considered. And Western man erects his own physical obstacles in his path. In sport we have bunkers, nets, hurdles, fences, ditches and so on, and training can be geared towards overcoming them or avoiding their traps. For the Japanese, the obstacle to overcome is no less than the devil within ourselves, that very devil which makes us shy away from success when we have it in sight, disbelieve our own worth or seek less than our potential deserves.

Students are not so much taught in Japan as guided. They are nudged gently along a path which will lead to the full understanding of what their own natures have to offer. They are not burdened with technical detail and they do not trouble about comparing themselves with others. For this reason they do not share the West's confidence in competition, although winning is no less important to them. Unlike Westerners, who need the stimulus of competition to bring out their best, the Japanese seem intimidated by it. Ruth Benedict, in her book *The Chrysanthemum and the Sword*, which has for many years been considered a highly influential book on the character of the Japanese, compares the results of tests showing the Western and Japanese attitudes towards competition:

We rely strongly on competition as a 'good thing'. Psychological tests show that competition stimulates us to our best work. Performance goes up under this stimulus; when we are given something to do all by ourselves we fall short of the record we make when there are competitors present. In Japan, however, their tests show just the opposite . . . With young men and adults performance deteriorated with competition. Subjects who had made progress reduced their mistakes and gained speed when they were working by themselves and began to make mistakes and were far slower when a competitor was introduced. They did best when they were measuring their improvement against their own record, not when they were measuring themselves against others. The Japanese experimenters rightly analysed the reason for this poor record in competitive situations. Their subjects, they said, when the project became competitive, became principally interested in the danger that they might be defeated, and the work suffered. They felt the competition so keenly as an aggression that they turned their attention to their relation to the aggressor instead of concentrating on the job in hand.

Karate, like many sports, is the gradual progress from one plateau to the next, each one requiring greater effort to reach. The higher the standard we reach, the longer time we seem to remain on the same level. Westerners find it difficult to come to terms with these stages, during which there seem to be few obvious signs of improvement, and may turn for consolation to their habits of competitiveness in an attempt to seek a tangible reward for their efforts. The Japanese may not even recognize these periods of apparent stagnation in their progress, basing their training, and indeed their more general outlook, on Nakayama's words: 'Karate-do is attained one step at a time, and so is life. Just train every day and try your best, and the truth will come to you.'

Karate is not exceptional in that it gets more demanding at the higher levels, not only because we have more background knowledge to call upon. It is not unusual for a student to feel further from 'mastering' the art after years of training than during the initial stages. For students, through learning how to defend themselves, must overcome the fact that by practising how to inflict injury they also become frighteningly aware of all the technical possibilities of how they themselves can be in danger.

Karlfried Graf Dürckheim describes in his book, *Hara: The Vital Centre of Man*, a point during his archery training when he was not allowed to stand still at a certain level of achievement:

I take up my position. The master stands before me . . . Before I have even reached the point where the arrow must touch the ear and cheek, and the bow is stretched to its fullest capacity, the deep voice of the master cuts right through me, 'Stop!' Surprised and a little irritated by this interruption at the moment of utmost concentration, I lower the bow. The master takes it from my hands, winds the string once round the end of the bow and hands it back to me smiling. 'Once again, please.' Unsuspecting, I begin again to go through the same series of motions. But when it comes to drawing the bow my strength fails me. The bow has now *twice* the tension it had before and my strength is insufficient. My arms begin to tremble. I sway unsteadily to and fro, the posture so painstakingly won is lost. The master, however, beings to laugh. Desperately I try again, but it is hopeless. Nothing but a pitiful failure. I must have looked rather vexed, for the master asks: 'What are you so annoyed about?' 'What? You can ask me that? For weeks and weeks I have practised and now, at the vital moment, you interrupt me before I have even drawn.' Once again the master laughs cheerfully, then suddenly serious, he says something like this: 'What exactly do you want? That you had accomplished the task I had given you I could see from the way you took up your bow. But the point is this — when a man, perhaps after a long struggle, has achieved a certain form in himself, in his life, in his work, only one misfortune can then befall him — that fate should allow him to stand still in that achievement. If fate means well by him it knocks his success out of his hands before it sets and hardens. To do just this during practice is the task of the good teacher. For what is the point of all this? Not the hitting of the target. For what ultimately matters, in learning archery or any other art, is not what comes out of it but what goes *into* it. Into, that is *into* the person . . . And what endangers this inner development more than anything else? Standing still in his achievement. A man must go on increasing, endlessly increasing.'

With this in mind it is possible to move way beyond the level at which most people stop.

KARATE AS A SPORT

At the critical moments of our lives it is the spirit and not the body that makes the rules. In sport the emphasis is on the strong body.

Judo provides the best example of an Eastern art which has detached itself from its original ideals. Sport judo has degenerated into little more than a calculated struggle to achieve results in contests based solely on physical strength and the well-honed use of a few favoured techniques. Karate has not so far declined to this level, particularly in Japan, but in the West the love of champions is so strong and the symbols of achievement so rooted in our nature that karate practised solely as a sport may in the future be irresistible.

The *dojos* (training halls), where the day-to-day practice of karate takes place, are often fairly unattractive places, or at least they are often venues such as church halls, youth and community centres hired on an *ad hoc* basis. It is not surprising, then, that some students are drawn towards the bright lights of Crystal Palace, the National Sports Centre, or other spacious arenas which house major tournaments. This contrast between types of venue is not unique to karate. Theatre groups, for example, may perform in well-equipped, often lavish, auditoriums, but they often rehearse in whatever rudimentary space is available to them.

In karate it is not so different outside Britain. The Japan Karate Association, before it moved to a converted bowling alley in the mid-1970s, had its headquarters in a shabby building in an area of Tokyo called Iidabashi. Despite its appearance the *dojo* had a strong functional and auspicious atmosphere. It was charged with a vitality reserved for places used solely for extreme physical activity. Yukio Mishima had lifted weights on the lower floor and had trained in the *dojo* up to black belt grade. In the changing room rows of *gis* (karate uniforms) hung from above and at various points along the walls, like washing hung out to dry in the back alleys of American tenement blocks. But these, although limp and stained with sweat, gave the impression of purpose. From here you could watch the instructors arrive at Suidobashi station and approach the building across a busy intersection. They stood out in the crowds, not because of their size but by the way they moved and their posture; an inner strength wrapped in outer silence. They seemed to be rooted to the ground by a centre of gravity lower than that found, or at least exhibited, in the West, where the emphasis on the upper body gives the walk of an athlete the impression of swagger. One was reminded of Kurosawa's film *Seven Samurai*, when the leader of the *samurai*, Kambie and the young, inexperienced Katsushiro were recruiting the men to protect the peasants' village from bandits. They were in a doorway or porch simply watching the passersby. Kambie was looking for something in particular; it was not an outward display of masculinity or defiance, but quite simply a way of walking, how the *samurai* were 'wearing' their strength within themselves while showing a calm and totally aware exterior. The young Katsushiro was unable to recognize that Kambie was looking for what the Japanese, even today, speak of as *hara no aru hito*, 'a man with belly' (see page 101).

No outdoor shoes, of course were allowed on the *dojo* floorboards, which almost shone from the daily polishing they received from the juniors. Either through age or the regular effects of earthquakes, the floor had become uneven; it undulated, just slightly, but enough to give it the effect of very gentle waves. The boards themselves creaked underfoot and were splintered at the edges. They had been taped up time and time again with long strips of wide, brightly-coloured tape, yellows, reds and greens, which gave a peculiar sense of gaiety to a place where one's spirit was put on the line. If you were lucky you avoided getting splinters in your feet, although you quickly learnt which areas to steer clear of.

Far removed from this was the Budokan, one of the most spectacular martial arts arenas in Japan and the venue for the All Japan Championships. Seats rise behind and above each other round a central open space in the style of a Greek amphitheatre. Competing in such a place would have represented to a Westerner a major pinnacle of achievement. But the day after a tournament the contestants, including the winners, would be back doing their regular basic training sessions on the uneven, taped-up boards of the *dojo* at Iidabashi, or similar places throughout Japan.

The high ideals of karate are rarely reflected in the venues at which it is taught. Nakayama has spoken of training on a small wooden deck outside Funakoshi Gichin's house, where there was room for only two people to practise at the same time, and even then they frequently bumped into each other. But the expectations of Westerners as regards places to do sport have been raised, not least by the march of the 'sport for all' concept, where well-equipped, glossy centres give sport a popular, even glamorous image. There may be a natural leaning towards karate as a sport, therefore, simply because it is in the more attractive venues that it displays its sporting side. But it must not be forgotten that it is in the modest church halls or on splintered, uneven *dojo* floors that the real work takes place.

Karate has so far avoided becoming an Olympic event. It may seem odd that the Japan Karate Association, if it were given the opportunity to take karate into the Olympics, would probably express reluctance to do so. Like the author who feels it is almost the kiss of death to be awarded the Nobel Prize, there is a feeling that something precious would be sacrificed. Generally, few things are elevated to a higher level just because they become popular. If karate were ever to become an Olympic event it would clearly gain prestige in the public eye, it would bring it directly into the area of competition, to which all sporting instincts could be applied and to which all spectators know how to respond. Apart from anything else, what would be on show would not be what karate aims to foster. But if it were to be well received as a valid Olympic event it would need to show itself capable of satisfying the needs of spectators, who generally applaud physical strength, but mistake it for personal or spiritual maturity. Karate would be misrepresented as a purely physical activity; all mental strengths would remain below the surface. It would be subjected to the partisanship of spectators and the excitement of commentators. All ritual and tradition would need to be abandoned. There may even come a time when only those nations which believed in the value of karate as an Olympic event would be represented, leaving the others to their practice on uneven floors in unglamorous *dojos*. Karate students could split into those who compete against each other in tournaments and those who compete with their own personal development; and spectators would only see karate's sporting front put on their benefit and believe it to be the real thing.

While writing this the Olympic Games in Korea were in progress. Taekwando, a Korean style of karate, was represented as a demonstration sport. No medals were at stake, but presumably to satisfy the requirements of competition there were winners and losers and competitors fought for points and half points as they do in all martial arts tournaments. The only piece of televised action broadcast in Britain showed a young man writhing on the floor having been kicked between the legs. It formed part of a light-hearted round-up of the less-fortunate competitors' setbacks during the day — horses throwing riders over fences, a diver hitting his head on the springboard and others whose mistakes were picked up by the cameras and relayed to the world. Beneficial it may be in terms of television viewer ratings, but Taekwando will live in the minds of the layman as being a 'sport' where young men with no control kick each other.

Karate, it must be remembered, is a martial art, and all the martial arts were thought of originally not as sporting pastimes or ways to keep fit, but as a way to preserve or take life. The vision was that wide; it was life or death. When those who professionally employed the martial arts, the *samurai*, came into contact with Zen they sought to absorb the mental attitudes into their day-to-day struggle to survive or kill while preserving their honour. However, this emphasis on actually killing an opponent fell away the more that Zen was absorbed, and the martial arts changed from being instruments of death into ways to look into one's own nature. So, to represent karate as a sporting conflict in a controlled, programmed tournament setting is little but empty imitation of the very thing martial arts had pulled away from.

When judo became an Olympic event in 1964 the Kodokan lost control. Judo liberated itself from its ideals as a martial way set down by Jigoro Kano (the founder of judo) and changed to fit the structure of the Olympics. Its original principles were jettisoned to the point where most students now train primarily to gain a competitive edge.

The wide visions of a martial art are lost when training for tournaments becomes the overriding motivation. Training becomes a calculated affair: strengths and weaknesses of opponents are taken into account and techniques practised to exploit their possible areas of vulnerability; the body is exercised according to a programme designed to make it 'peak' at the time of a contest and relax afterwards; a limited number of favoured moves are perfected specifically for use under tournament conditions. Preparing for a tournament may give some students a sense of purpose to their regular training sessions, which may seem to offer little reward for their efforts without the focus on a future time when their 'skill' will be put to the test. Other students may feel that the next grading is enough of a target to aim for. In each case their fate is postponed in the present and will be determined, one way or the other, in the future. Their lives oscillate between calm and activity, between which they live more or less in limbo. It is noticeable, for example, that some *dojos* are often well attended just before tournaments or gradings and thinly populated immediately afterwards.

Karate demands that we devote ourselves wholly to every moment of our lives, whatever it is we are doing, however meaningful or mundane. While doing such things as walking, eating, working or talking, what could be called a karate-mind must be consciously maintained. In terms of external threats, any moment can bring our downfall; we never know what the next second of our lives will be like. And for those gearing their training and their lives around tournaments, major threats may occur during their preparations, before their bodies have 'peaked', when they are relaxed and vulnerable.

This concentration on the present moment is crucial in regular training sessions within a *dojo*. Every technique must be performed as though it were the last, nothing must be kept in reserve; there should be complete tensing of the muscles on completion of a movement and full relaxation afterwards. This is in keeping with one of the very basic philosophies of all the martial arts — there is no second chance. In any conflict, the person who believes there is a second chance will always lose against the person who believes his first chance is also his last. We are thrown back again to times when the martial arts really did mean life or death; two men faced each other and one was going to die. It was simple and intense. Time and again we can see the original principles of karate and the martial arts spilling over into the lives of modern man. We equip ourselves in the same way as the past only if we remain loyal to these basic principles and confront our world, different as it is but no less demanding. If we don't we become almost strangers on the earth, as though by choice we hibernate from it, emerging only for training sessions, gradings and tournaments.

Among the number of basic movements which make up
the technical system of karate there are some which seem
to us reasonably straightforward from the start and others
which seem impossible. It may simply be that our bodies
are more suited to some positions than to others. (The
activities called 'physical education' in our schools may
help to improve all-round physical strength and
coordination, but as the emphasis is on the upper part of
the body our feeling for many of the basic movements in
karate is at first too high.) The natural tendency is to
cultivate strengths and neglect weaknesses. But our
success in karate, to a large extent, depends on how
directly we confront these weaknesses, for it is these
that poison our overall ability if they are continuously
ignored.

This state of affairs is further increased if we
concentrate on only a few favourite techniques in
preparation for tournaments. Any athlete who competes in
an event made up of several disciplines — a swimming
medley, the decathlon — neglects one discipline only at his
or her peril. Some, of course, they will be better at than
others, but none will be weak. And so with karate, the
difference being that if we disregard any area of weakness
we do not just lose a sporting contest but often render
ourselves defenceless. There is always in a contest the
possibility that we will come up against an opponent who
has made a speciality of countering our favourite attack.
But, because karate has to distort itself so much to fit the
structure of tournaments, it is equally possible that
competitors' weaknesses may not be found out, and
successful competitors may be lulled into thinking that
they have high overall ability. They get a distorted image
of their resources if their one or two favourite techniques
'come off' on the day. What is worse, because it may be
their lives at risk rather than their egos, is that they may
only be able to respond under tournament conditions.
Taken to an extreme, a tournament champion, having
limited his resources to a few carefully developed
techniques, may not be able to defend himself in real life.

In Tokyo in 1964 the Dutchman, Anton Geesink, from Utrecht, won the Olympic gold medal in the open judo event. He was the favourite to win, already having twice won the World Championships, the first non-Japanese ever to do so. His victories caused an uproar in Japan, for he so efficiently swept aside all Japanese opposition in their own art. According to Nakayama, the Chief Instructor of the Japan Karate Association, plans were made to study Geesink's secrets of competition, and a Japanese journalist was commissioned to interview him to discover the training methods used. Geesink's reply is a strong indictment of the system which consciously breeds competitors in the martial arts.

The Japanese have devoted themselves to the study of judo for competitions. They have gone to extraordinary lengths to develop winning contestants and fine champions. I, on the other hand, have never trained for competition in my life. All I have ever done is trained in judo as a way of life, exactly as Dr Kano taught. While the Japanese were devising competitive strategies, I was in the *dojo*, practising basics and *kata*. I defeated the Japanese because I know judo better than the Japanese. The secret is to train every day in the basics. This will make you unbeatable.

There is no suggestion in all the above, that sport is not fun — it is exhilarating to take part in and nail-biting to watch. And there are some feelings that only athletes can experience. But in the extreme physical sports, an athlete's ability to compete at high levels is limited to a narrow age range — the body grows too old to withstand the rigours of sport beyond a certain age. For students who have practised karate only as a sport, this limits their years of involvement in an art which, under normal circumstances, can reasonably be expected to endure for life.

KARATE AS AN ART

From what has been said above, it should be clear why most students of karate in the West, at least those who are relatively new to it, regard it as a sport. It is likely that they practise it as though it were a sport — and so, for them at least, it is. The associations which sport conjures up in most people's minds revolve around leisurely relaxation, healthy tension, competition and a way to keep fit, alert and coordinated. Above all, though, sport for most people means enjoyment. Karate unquestionably is all of these things, so there is nothing seriously wrong, at least on the surface, in regarding it too as sport. However, it is clear that it is more, or offers more, than the commonly recognized sporting activities. Some students may regard karate as sport so as to ensure that they are actively involved in a world that is enjoyable, rather than something serious for which they have to steal themselves and approach with different motivations. The paradox is that most people, although they think of sport as being enjoyable, involve themselves in it with obsessive seriousness. Sport indeed should be fun, but the great danger is to get so swept up in it that the tight-lipped seriousness of competing contaminates all elements of enjoyment.

The passing of time and people's changing attitudes inevitably have a major influence on such activities, as in the case of sport judo. It is hard now to see any signs of sport judo's martial beginnings. It submits itself to all the conditions and restrictions applying to competitive sport, so that judo players may find themselves sitting in line with synchronized swimmers still wet from the pool and footballers caked with mud, all waiting to give blood samples for drug analysis. Indeed, the first British competitor to be disqualified from an Olympic event for drug abuse was a judo player. Judo as a martial art may, then, be at its lowest ebb, but judo as a sport is now a serious affair.

Sport in whatever form is ultimately valueless in terms

of human development unless we think of physical fitness as being more than what it is. Being able to run quickly round in circles, to lift heavy weights or to throw something a long way does not necessarily mean that the athlete is an improved person or even that he or she is very nice at all. But we in the West have such a high regard for sporting achievement that we rarely look beyond it to the human folly involved. In some cases we even feel smugly satisfied when we find that an athlete of high sporting ability has failings equal to our own. Excessively childish behaviour or petty tantrums can even be thought of as a normal part of an athlete's make-up, as this tends to raise even higher his or her level of achievement, for it shows that a high personal sacrifice is being made to achieve success. So we tolerate the coarsest of behaviour on the sports fields and tennis courts in the name sport, which would be thought of as intolerably vulgar in everyday life.

The Japanese, on the other hand, judge all human endeavour and achievement not on results or public opinion but on evidence of inner maturity. Most people can spend years of their life developing a high skill which to the untrained may seem miraculous, but if the techniques are built on shallow motives of pride, greed, insincerity and so on, they have, for the Japanese, no value whatsoever. If you take a young boy of five or six and encourage him to swing round bars every day in the style of a chimpanzee, he will be able to swing round bars very well by the time he is 16 and will be awarded points for his technique in the Olympics. In terms of inner substance, however, his technical skill probably means very little. In the case of one of the martial or traditional Japanese arts, such training would be thought to have failed, for the Japanese arts do not divorce inner development of the person from the technical results. To them, personal quality is measured by as near perfect external result as possible which shines through from a deep inner harmony. This is not to say that Japanese arts are more distinguished than those in the West, or that Western sports and arts pale by comparison. On the contrary, what is considered as art in the East can reveal itself in visually very small objects or quite insubstantial activities. Sometimes there is nothing in terms of a tangible object to show as a result; such things as questions and answers in Zen, military strategy and the tea ceremony can all be classified as art because they can all be subject to the same laws as the higher arts and lead to personal inner harmony. It is more a matter of *doing* something perfectly rather than *creating* something of perfection; the 'artist' is actually making a work of art out of himself, not something for the admiration or gratification of an audience. In the West, though, it is the regard for the actual object created that will determine the success or failure of the artist, no matter in what spirit it was created and no matter what personal or social sacrifices were made during the making process. The artist can be quite incidental, which begs the question whether activities and arts in the West can still be seen as high achievement if the sportsman or artist is known, for example, to be a tearaway, child-beater or bully in everyday life.

In karate, as in the other Eastern arts, any sign of inner turmoil is thought to tarnish all the externalized activities or objects of creation which emanate from it. The person concerned should have made no personal or social sacrifices for the sake of what is performed or created, at least to the extent that his or her character should not have suffered as a result. Instead the activities gain value only when the person concerned actually lives the knowledge gained and expresses it in outer behaviour in everyday life. Karate, therefore, or any of the other arts, should never become an end in itself. Superficialities and everything superfluous should be allowed to fall away, leaving the person to perform in a spirit of purity rather than in circumstances where he or she is at odds with their own personality. It is this which identifies karate, at least in the Japanese interpretation of the word, as an art.

The Western nations, through encouragement or coercion, have been conditioned to walk tall, to stand with chest out, stomach in and shoulders pulled back; in other words to give emphasis to the upper part of the body. Above all, though, we believe that all high achievement is the more or less direct product of intellectual or rational endeavours.

There is a fundamental split in the West between the powers of the head and the powers of the body. The body is seen only as a vehicle for the mind. This marks one of the greatest contrasts between the Western cultures and traditional Eastern attitudes towards the mind and body. For the Eastern traditions assert that the physical and mental, the male and female, spirit and matter, the restful Yin and the active Yang, combine to form a dynamic balance leading to man's harmonious existence, standing as he does between heaven and earth. Expressed in physical terms the harmony of man's world relies on his appreciation of the unity between the upper and lower parts of the body; that is, between his head and his stomach. For those of us involved in the martial arts the balance between the physical and mental elements must be resolved; how do we free ourselves from our intellectual bonds and put a higher value on 'nature working within us'? There is no problem here of karate students getting bogged down by an over-emphasis on spiritual matters; unlike some of the martial arts such as archery, there is always the possibility of an opponent jolting them back to full physical alertness. On the other hand, those who deny any attachment to the mental aspects of karate at worst regard what they are doing as an instrument of aggression, which usually means it is a concentrated extension of their everyday lives, or at best attain a certain degree of technical skill comparable to a sort of mechanical or martial exercise.

It is natural that we should cling doggedly to the rational, deductive sphere of our lives, which we believe we have a certain amount of control over and which seems to serve us so well in all other areas of our lives, rather than submit ourselves to something mysterious and seemingly beyond our control. The Japanese character *kara* in *karate*, meaning 'empty' or 'void', not only implies being free from bad intentions or distractions from the outside world, but detached from the mindfulness and intentional impulses promoted by rational thoughts. Some people may feel unequal to the task of 'rendering themselves empty' of their intellectual rational urges, as it may suggest an abandonment of all independent avenues of self-expression and a very real threat to personal values. What makes life colourful and absorbing to them is the very human faculty of the mind and the personal idiosyncrasies which go with it, and to surrender these to an 'inner mystique' which is at once unknown and irrational would be to rob life of an essential human resource. It would put an intolerable burden on their approach to life and be counter to everything they believe they stand for, amounting to a dislocation in personal habits and instincts. Certainly it is uncomfortable to confront our restlessness, instability and self-deceptions, which cause us to run headlong from one distraction to another or to tumble uncaringly through life hardly ever really satisfied with it or with ourselves. But karate and the other martial arts, when properly approached, require us to take the risk of leaping into unknown realms where we find out what we knew all along, that all artificial distractions lead nowhere in the end. What matters for students of karate, if they wish to progress beyond a mere mechanical skill, is for them to relinquish all the superfluous elements of their lives which they covet but which they really know are leading them astray.

It goes without saying that is is important to reflect on our performance after each training session and to analyse our mistakes and strengths. At the very end of each period of practice there is therefore a short period of meditation, called *moksu*, where the whole class in a kneeling, relaxed position concentrate on their breathing with eyes closed. During these times each student can examine their own performance during the class from a technical point of view and reflect on his or her own state of mind. These brief, concentrated periods consolidate the students' relationship with their training, and are significantly the final few moments of each session before the students go out of the *dojo* and into the world outside. The implied function, then, is for students to think about how their training can benefit themselves and others outside the *dojo* rather than readmit into their lives their everyday cares.

The issue here is not to empty ourselves of all rational thoughts concerning training generally, but to dismiss intentional thinking which precedes actions and responses of physical movement. Technical mastery of karate movements are clearly of prime importance; they are the foundation upon which everything else is built. But under no circumstances must they be performed in a way that suggests they are an agent of the mind and the conscious will. In other words, a point must be reached that is beyond technique, where all movements 'happen' naturally, unintentionally and effortlessly, just as a bird flaps its wings or an eye blinks at a fly's approach. All the Ways proceed to this point, where there is no gap between thought and action — the action, whether it is a karate movement, the release of an arrow, a brush stroke, happens on its own, without the mediation of thought. And all actions which result from this thoughtless spontaneity have a special richness and naturalness free from man's impurities. In contrast, when the mind is instigating a series of movements each one will be seen, even by the layman, to be an artificially constructed fragment of the whole, for when the mind involves itself with action it separates combinations of movements into their individual parts which, when performed, are without natural fluidity and spontaneity. This is particularly noticeable in the performance of karate *katas*, which involve the continuous flow of movements, sometimes upwards of 60, containing very fast and very slow movements, techniques requiring balance and muscular control combined with rapid changes of direction and realignment of the body's centre of gravity. A *kata* performed as it should be is a series of individual techniques, each one consciously and painstakingly practised and then performed as a single, flowing and unconscious act. When the mind intrudes upon the movements, however, they not only lose their natural flow so that all dynamism is lost but the person performing the *kata* more often than not forgets the movements altogether or gets hopelessly muddled. As well as this, the person labours for breath during the *kata* and is pathetically breathless at the end, as the synchronization of breathing and moving has been seriously disrupted. It is as though the mind, in its attempt to help, actually muddies the issue.

Where the mind prompts an action the proper moment for the action is usually lost. In Japanese archery, for instance, when the archer draws the bow at full stretch the tip of the arrow oscillates, very slightly but enough to make the difference between hitting and missing the target. The archer must 'decide' at what moment to release the arrow. If the decision is conscious and the message from the brain 'tells' the fingers to release the arrow, the arrow tip would have moved further round its oscillation cycle and the moment for accurate release is lost. We in the West may see this as an opportunity to come to terms intellectually with this gap between thinking and response, in this case thinking about releasing the arrow and actually doing it, by 'cheating' the oscillation of the arrow tip. By rationally examining the time it takes between the thought and the action we could actually allow for the arrow tip's travel around its oscillation cycle and therefore be more certain of hitting the target. The person whose calculations are most accurate would achieve the most hits, win the contest and that would be the end of the matter. This principle can be applied to all sports, especially those where the time between thought and response can be intellectually used to a player's advantage. It marks an important distinction between sport, which is mostly to do with technique, and the world of creative 'non-thinking' which lies beyond.

From whatever our standpoint, all true art transcends purely technical ability; it must emanate from the region beyond technique. By making such rational adjustments, as in the case of the arrow tip's oscillation, we can perhaps achieve a high degree of perfection, but our performance would remain as sport, albeit on a high level of purely outward mechanical skill. However, hitting the target is not the ultimate goal for the Japanese archer, although, of course, continuously missing indicates a flaw in technique or mental distraction. Archer, bow and target must merge into one harmonious whole, where the archer is loosing the shot acts without doing, without intention. If he 'cheats' the arrow tip's oscillation, even if this means he is more likely to hit the target 'intellectually', an unnatural vibration of the bow occurs and with it is removed the inner contentment of the archer. Needless to say, any chance hits are seen as failures.

In karate, too, not only does the intentional will limit students to technical skills it creates what can be considered a fatal moment of hesitation prior to action. As karate assumes an opponent who must at all times be thought of as an actual adversary, it is the student's responsibility and aim to reduce the period of hesitation to nil. All karate training should regard this as the ultimate objective and be geared towards it. Only in this way will our welfare lie within ourselves rather than with the opponent. And surely, some may say, this is the whole point of it all. There is no opportunity, of course, for 'cheating' a target in karate as there is in archery, as the momentary hesitation, if it exists at all, can be, and inevitably is, our undoing.

We can try to get around it by anticipating what an opponent will do, but the only sure approach is to get to a point in training where we respond naturally and without thinking to an opponent's technique once he or she is completely committed to it. Anticipation in any sport is likely to lead to failure. The body in all matters follows the mind. So when the mind 'fixes' itself on a possible action, the body prepares itself to respond and usually responds too soon. When there is even the slightest deviation from what is expected, the mind has to make adjustments to 're-fix' on the new action and therefore gives the body insufficient time to respond. Hans Joachim Stein, in *Kyudo: The Art of Zen Archery*, sums this up when talking about a man who has become 'empty' to the point where he responds naturally to any situation:

> Unimpeded by any manifestation of the outer consciousness he dwells in 'total awareness'. The state of perfect mindfulness allows him to grasp the essence of all things directly without the mediation of discursive thought. On that basis, his actions will be spontaneous and in perfect accordance with the demands of whatever the situation may be. His mental state of emptiness and purity is in harmony with all the conditions of daily existence, which keeps him from losing touch with reality and treating life as a kind of exercise in metaphysics. His body has become an instrument to be used by the cosmic energies at work in him, just as he himself can make instrumental use of these cosmic energies.

These 'cosmic energies', thought to be present in everybody, are what the Japanese attempt to uncover and are what the conscious mind of a student or any intentional effort tends to obscure. In order to break down the layers of consciousness, which prompt the body's movements in karate, or more accurately, to let these layers fall away naturally, a student will spend years of continuous training, repeating movements over and over again, with and without an opponent, aiming in the end to allow techniques to flow freely from his 'deepest inner centre'. All training must lead ultimately towards this point, where techniques simply happen, without volition. Only then will they be performed with the natural sureness which goes with unintentionality.

At first all techniques will be practised consciously until skill is finally perfected — this is the initial aim. From this technical platform the students to some extent should 'let go' of technique, in the sense that they should become less conscious of it, for it is at this stage that they can perceive how much desire, ambition, pride, fear and so on obstruct their path. Then the work on themselves can begin. It is only at this stage that practice in the real sense truly begins, after the period of conscious application to the technical skills has produced in the student a foundation of physical ability. Even the names of karate grades reflect this. During the initial stages the grades start from ninth *kyu* and work down to first *kyu*; after that the black belt grades start from first *dan* and work upwards — the Japanese use *shodan, nidan* and so on, for the grades of black belt, meaning 'first step', 'second step', etc. The *kyu* grades indicate that the students work on technique, while the *dan* grades show that they work on themselves. It is not, of course, this clearcut, for there is no cut-off point where the students switch from consciously practising technique to turn their practice in upon themselves. In all the martial arts technique comes first and then mental awareness — the two must form a unity. For example, D.T. Suzuki, in his book *Zen and Japanese Culture*, which has become an almost indispensable guide to the Japanese arts, talks about the association of technique and mind in swordsmanship:

> The secrets of perfect swordsmanship consist in creating a certain frame or structure of mentality which is made always ready to respond instantly to what comes from outside. While technical training is of great importance, it is after all something artificial, consciously, calculatingly added and acquired. Unless the mind that avails itself of the technical skill somehow attunes itself to a state of the utmost fluidity or mobility, anything acquired or superimposed lacks spontaneity of natural growth.

It should by now be clear that continuous effort and practice rather than continuous knowledge and thinking is the way to overcome the most persistent obstacle in the students' path, that is the students themselves. It is for this reason that training sessions concentrate on actual physical practice with little or no time spent on theoretical discussions or even, at least at first, on the significance or application of the movements; the students naturally discover this for themselves.

The meaning of practice, then, from a Japanese point of view, is penetrating beyond the outer layers of conscious thought and everyday distractions to a person's 'inner centre'. The more students open themselves to the way of practice the more important it is for them to realize what they can in fact achieve through it. However much students have become estranged from this 'inner centre', the forces within them, through constant practice, will heal and integrate them and pull them back to the path through which they can rediscover themselves and build on their consciously acquired technical skills. Only by clinging to outer distractions, by not 'letting go' of themselves, will students resist the natural forces which are constantly at work within them. Dürckheim talks of practice as meaning ultimately 'learning to let the in-dwelling reality of Being emerge', in other words to allow all obstacles to our true selves fall away.

> Being is ever at work trying to break through man's shell and to enter the light of his consciousness. Fundamentally this urge of life towards the light is the primal force behind all human life and activity, but if the only channel it can find in a man runs through a hard ego-shell it will be choked and blocked.

If we accept this, then the logical conclusion is that a person who acts without premeditation, without intention and free from everyday cares and motivations is not ultimately responsible for his or her own actions. But as technical movements are performed with natural purity if the performer is empty of external thoughts, so will everyday conduct and behaviour accord with the ethical foundations which the martial arts aim to promote. The *dojo* code (see pages 73-74), which students in many *dojos* say after each training session, intends to foster in the students a responsibility towards humaneness, propriety and sincerity which are thought to be inevitable if they shine through from a person's inner, natural centre.

Rational thinking and intentional effort which cloud the path to our 'inner centre' cannot be reduced by rational or intentional means. For the last refuge for our intentional will is thought to be the intention to 'get rid of it'. For the karate student the falling away of personal obstacles to progress happens quite naturally over the years, providing persistent and continuous physical effort is maintained. Unlike many of the traditional Eastern arts and practices, such as yoga and meditation, karate is not contemplative, it is physical. Training works on levels where severe demands are put on the body and the spirit by taking students to the brink of physical exhaustion, where the workings of the mind give way and where the spirit reaches out to new horizons. At the same time the body tries to keep a grasp on the principle forms of technique. By constant repetition the body knows what it should do, and the more established the technique the more stubbornly the body resists giving way to exhaustion. In many ways students' technical skills are determined by how well they manage to hold on to technique when their body is constantly being put under such strenuous demands. A student's energies are channelled more into the region of the spirit, which is the body's ally, leaving him or her with little scope for maintaining intellectual links with the physical movements. In this way, then, karate's physical emphasis is essential for students in their efforts to rid themselves of extraneous thoughts or intentional impulses, for the task of 'rendering themselves empty' is taken out of their hands by a system that involves constant physical training.

Whatever discipline we decide to practise, if it is worth doing it will be strenuous and relentless. In karate and the other martial and traditional arts, training should be approached without the compulsion of wanting to achieve anything. Continuous practice involves the gradual build-up of technical skills along with a gradual falling away of mental and personal obstacles. It is a process that cannot be rushed, and there are no short cuts. Even the determination to work and train hard, if that involves impatience or personal ambition, is thought to be a hindrance to progress, as it represents a manifestation of the outer ego. This is illustrated by an anonymous Zen anecdote which claims that 'When one eye is fixed upon your destination, there is only one eye left with which to find the Way'.

Another old Zen anecdote about swordsmanship, equally applicable to karate or any of the other martial arts, tells of a young man who went to a great master to learn the art of swordsmanship. The master, who was in retirement in his mountain hut, agreed to take on the young man as a student. The young man assured the master that he was ready to work hard and asked how long it would take him to master the art. At least ten years, replied the master. This seemed like an intolerably long time to the young man, so he emphasized that he was prepared to apply himself to the task day and night. It would therefore take at least thirty years, replied the master. The young man stressed that he was willing to spare himself no effort and was prepared to summon up all his strength and devote every moment of his life to perfecting the art. In that case, replied the master, it would probably take at least 70 years.

The young man gave up his questions and entrusted himself to the master. For three years he cooked rice, gathered wood, made fires, swept the hut and meditated, but was not even allowed to hold a sword. So he approached the master and asked him when his teaching was to begin. From then on, whenever the young man was doing his chores, the master would approach and strike him from behind with a wooden sword. The surprise attacks were repeated at frequent but unpredictable periods, whenever the young man was busy and his attention was on his work. At first the young man could do nothing with any peace of mind, as he never knew when or from which direction he may be struck by the master. After a time, though, he began to avoid the blows instinctively, until his body eventually responded naturally and spontaneously without the intervention of his mind or will.

The anecdote ends with the master cooking his own vegetables in a pan over an open fire. Seizing his opportunity, the young man took up the wooden sword and aimed it at the back of the master's head. But the sword was caught by the master in the cover of the pan. At that moment the young man for the first time appreciated the unparalleled kindness of the master, for his initial preparation in the art of the sword had been allowed to grow within him, his body and mind had been awakened to full consciousness, so his real training in the art could begin.

And so, too, with karate, where the feeling for one's body and spontaneous, intuitive physical action emerges naturally, if we let it, over a period of time — 'It is just a matter of letting the master who is in us come out.'

PART 3 PRACTICAL ASPECTS

THE STUDENT

There are now many different styles of karate. Some are the so-called 'soft' styles, others are 'hard'. This is not a difference of difficulty, but concerns more the technical mechanics involved — the 'hard' styles use the explosive power of the body from a state of complete rest to that of complete, but sudden and momentary, tenseness (*kime*), whereas the 'soft' styles often use circular and continuously flowing movements. Karate can also be classified according to the country or place of origin, mainly Japan, China, Okinawa and Korea. Although the reference section at the back of the book gives pointers towards the main styles and systems which exist in Britain, the substance of this book concerns the Japanese style called *Shotokan*. The reason for this was not only to prevent the book becoming a sort of kaleidoscope of detail without a central focus, but because *Shotokan* is the most widespread style in Britain and is thought by many to be essentially the most graceful and effective and the one least spoilt or tarnished by time. It is also felt to suit the body and the spirit of the Westerner best.

Karate does not involve weapons. Some techniques are practised, particularly in the *katas*, which are defences against such things as sticks and poles, but students themselves remain unarmed at all times. Armed 'opponents' are imagined, not real. (Students should have the right to leave if such things as knives are ever introduced into a *dojo*.) Breaking blocks of wood, bricks, roof tiles and so on is also taboo. Nothing in a *dojo* is hit apart from the *makiwara* (see page 78) and empty air. Students only usually touch when one attacks with a part of the body and the other blocks it. It is unusual, too, for karate students to be thrown or pulled to the ground: there is no tugging a partner's *gi* or grappling, and there are no strangleholds as there are in judo. Students of karate practise on their feet, either one or both, shifting their weight from one stance to another and at all times using the stomach to maintain balance and power and to root them to the ground. Karate, then, at its best, can be as elegant as, say, a gymnastic floor exercise, if not more so, as there is a vibrancy and energy which radiates from the body when it is operating at high speed and alternating between the extremes of relaxation and tenseness.

When beginners first step on to the *dojo* floor the assumption is that they know nothing, they are essentially empty vessels, which is why the first thing to be learnt is the natural way to stand, *shizen-tai*, how to make a fist by folding in the fingers tightly and binding them strongly with the thumb, and the first and most basic stance, *zenkutsu-dachi*, the front stance. The student will repeat over and over again these and other basic movements, yet even after years they will often not feel quite right. But they are like the letters of an alphabet, which form meaningful words in combinations of techniques and which flourish into an expressive, moving prose in the *katas*. Little by little the student lays a basic foundation upon which later his skill will depend. Much is to be won or lost here. As a baby's life is said to be forged within the first 30 days or so, so too the karate student's technique. A world that is different is discovered, full of unlimited opportunities which are within reach but which have to be earned right from the very beginning. Karate does not simply sink in, and it is not absorbed through the pores like a constantly repeated child's verse; it is carved out of our reluctant bone and muscle which ache when we are training and often when we are not.

Improvement in karate is the student's responsibility; in Japan those who are lazy or slack are not punished but ignored (although lack of etiquette is severely dealt with). All too often an advanced karate student's grade makes claims on his technique which he cannot measure up to as faults in the very basic movements are revealed. If a basic technique is not mastered at the beginning, then later the only worthwhile thing to do is to scrap what exists and start again — break down the technique and rebuild from scratch, in the same way that an otherwise worthy student in Japan who develops a conceited attitude is broken down so that a new, fresh spirit can emerge. Quite often students are over-eager to get to the first grade, which can be taken after two months, and so miss the valuable opportunity they have to perfect the very basic movements and so become, in a sense, masters of themselves. It seems harsh and non-productive, but after black belt gradings in Japan the very next lesson is a return to the absolute basics which were introduced in the first few weeks of training. Even after the All Japan Championships, competitors return the next day to very basic techniques, for without first mastering these one can only get to a certain level and no further. In the same way, one can go only so far in a foreign language if only a few words of vocabulary are known.

Students then develop the way to move, with hips low, head still and back straight. Always relaxing the shoulders and centring their mind in their stomach, and always pushing the feeling of the body forward, concentrating on straight lines. From the start there should be no eccentric facial expressions, no outward displays of discomfort, spirit, exhaustion. It all happens on the inside and is expressed through pure, clean movement.

The learning curve at first is steeper than it will ever be, simply because there is so much to learn — the techniques themselves and their Japanese names, how to breathe properly, the stances and, above all, the first *kata, heian shodan.* (In some organizations an even simpler kata, called *kihon,* 'basic', has been introduced.) Through the exercises the hips become more mobile and better able to twist into movements or push outward or forward, with the stomach always as the controlling centre. The ankles become more flexible and less tense. Students perform in lines up and down the *dojo,* hearing their breath, feeling the response of their bodies; with this *habit* is learnt, not just the rules. They will sometimes practise in pairs and feel how the twist of a punch can be blocked by a twist of the forearm and how the body, if allowed, adjusts distance and has a natural tendency to protect itself against anything that is propelled towards it. Later, perhaps much later, they will cease to feel that *they* are moving their bodies at all, there will be nothing between the will and the act. Only through constant repetition can this be achieved, but, at those rare, fleeting moments, it will all seem so worthwhile.

The movements of the first *kata* are first practised a movement at a time, then built up until all the 21 movements fit together to form one complete exercise. Over and over again the students establish the sequence of movements, until their bodies cannot take the wrong direction. At this stage, it is all consciously approached, for all through the *kyu* grades it is technique that is foremost. And the movements are all very simple, in that no flamboyance or fussiness should detract from the precise, clear lines.

Students will learn through the *kata* that karate has nothing to do with brute force — it is elegant, graceful and dynamic. It also becomes clear that it could be highly effective. And if it is, could it not be used against the students themselves? By becoming familiar with techniques that could harm others, students after a time consider the possibility of the same techniques, or those similarly effective, being used by others. Their initial enthusiasm and openness can be blunted by such thoughts and stealthy fingers of self-doubt can take hold — their mind undercuts the confidence they have in their bodies. Many give way to anxiety and stop training at this stage, as the initial rush of knowledge becomes to them a sort of overbearing liability. Others take on the air of confidence that often afflicts those who know very little about something, but enough to impress those who know nothing. All such thoughts and gestures must be discarded — karate is a long journey and the way is faster and more comfortable without them. There are plenty of periods during training when improvement seems to desert students altogether; the steep learning curve at the beginning tails off and one seems almost to standstill in ability. There is a tendency at these stages to find a cause, and make adjustments, and often to over-compensate. Instead of concentrating on ourselves when practising with a partner we just try to make it difficult for the other person, as though our ability, rather than being forged out of our own bodies and minds, can be built on the mistakes of others. But students must go onward, ever onward, exploring areas they never thought they could reach, so that finally they will never do anything that is beyond them. It is as though they push themselves to climb Everest or the Eiger and yet, even at the most critical moments of everyday life, they only ever have to walk up Snowdon.

After a time training becomes a solitary, private journey. Most karate students who reach a certain standard remain silent about it, sometimes even for years, not through aloofness or in any sense of them having renounced the outside world, but because karate becomes a personal struggle that is not easily shared with those on the fringe. But it reaches out into all other areas of one's life — into other sports and activities and into one's general outlook. Even when we walk or talk or just sit, it is there, ever-present. Students can turn their backs on karate whenever they wish, they can leave as freely as they entered, but karate will never turn its back on a student. In a world that so often disappoints, karate can be relied on, stable and never changing. Despite being a hard system of destruction, karate, paradoxically, leads to gentleness. It tempers aggressive instincts and smooths down the rough edges of a violent nature. Students aim to be unassuming, avoiding conflict where possible with smiling indifference, for karate is believed to begin and end with courtesy. When it is absolutely necessary to fight it is never necessary to intimidate, but to disarm or win quickly and without fuss and with no self-congratulation afterwards, for when a karate student hits another person he essentially hits himself.

The early stages of karate can perhaps best be summed up by a student in the early years of training. In response to a questionnaire, the following was received from an 18-year-old student (from the *Tora* club in Woking) who had been training for two-and-a-half years and had reached fifth *kyu* (purple belt). The question asked was 'What do you like and dislike about karate?'

What I like about karate is seeing myself improve, although I rarely detect it. What I dislike is the hard training needed to improve. Sometimes I hate it. I can explain this best by a conversation I had with my grandmother. She asked one day, 'Which karate night do you think is best?' I replied 'Fridays definitely.' Then she said, 'That's the one you enjoy the most, I suppose.' I replied, 'No, that's the one I hate!' She looked quite confused.

I think I feel apprehensive because karate makes you take a good look at yourself, or another way of putting it is to say you are testing yourself to find out your true capabilities, or whether you're a success or a failure. I guess I'm apprehensive of discovering the latter.

THE DOJO

A *dojo* can literally be any enclosed space used by students as a 'place of the Way'. In the West few clubs are so economically well-established as to be able to set up and run a permanent *dojo*, so most are small church halls, sports and community centres and so on hired for the days of training.

Traditional Japanese *dojos* would have wooden floors, perhaps a mirror and several *makiwaras* (punching boards). As far as possible, natural materials would be preferred. At the entrance there would be a place where all outdoor shoes are left, as symbolically the outside world stops at the threshold. Most importantly, nothing should attract the eye of the student or call attention to itself. Essentially, then, it is a free, open space to which students arrive with free, open minds.

A *dojo* should neither be an extension of the outside world nor a sanctuary from it where students take occasional refuge, but a place of intense physical and mental activity where students behave intensively and then leave to take a more active and rewarding part in society outside. The practice which goes on inside a *dojo* is considered a microcosm of life. Preferably a *dojo* should be silent, but where there is diverting noise students hear nothing but their own breath, and where there is distracting clutter students should see nothing but the empty space around them, occupied by an imaginary enemy. It is one of the few places where people can honestly regard the free space they are in as inviolable. The general effect is to endow the place with a special vitality which rubs off on those who enter and clings to them when they leave.

Students come to a *dojo* with humility, willing to accept instruction as though voluntarily cornered for a personal test. A 'club' atmosphere often exists in *dojos*, so students feel loyal to themselves as well as to others, assuming they are sincere. A united reaction may rise, therefore, against the hot-headed show-off or the street thug who strays in from outside. The place becomes special and students respond protectively to it as though beholden to it for what it offers them. There is also a no-nonsense feeling of willing commitment, which allows little room for personal mannerism, prejudice, innuendo, strutting and so on which embellish the sports fields and places of practice elsewhere.

PURITY

In the East the unspoken assumption in all the arts is that whatever is physical is also spiritual — they stand as a path to self-knowledge. In the West we choose to take up one of the more physical Japanese arts — karate, judo, aikido, etc. — usually because it *is* physical and may even question the relevance of any spiritual emphasis at all. A Japanese taking up karate would quite naturally see the spiritual and physical elements as inseparable, forming an organic unity leading along a path to self-maturity. They would bring with them from the start the understanding that what they were doing was a mere instrument through which they become conscious of themselves. A Westerner, on the other hand, at first may not even consider the spiritual side and would regard what they were doing as a complete end in itself. The point is that the Japanese assume that there are many enemies to combat within themselves, while Westerners wish to prepare a defence against possible threats from the world at large. In a seemingly hostile world we seek ways of making ourselves feel more secure; the Japanese, however, viewing the pressure of the world as constantly pulling them away from the true essence of their nature, seek activities and arts to bring them back to it. In all cases, however, it is doubtful that anyone who persists in the rigorous training that karate demands will avoid, at some stage, having to look themselves in the eye.

Negative characteristics often assert themselves in students, particularly after the initial period spent getting to grips with the basic technical elements. Negative characteristics are thought of as cutting people off from their 'true natures', rather than constituting a basis for improvement. Karate conforms to all other Eastern ways of thinking in that it does not aim to build on the existing personal make-up of the individual or even directly to turn negative characteristics — conceit, competitiveness, greed, etc. — into positive qualities such as self-confidence, generosity and so on. Indeed, layers of habit, desires, ambition, etc. must be peeled away to reveal an inner purity which is thought to exist beneath the surface in everyone and which shines through into general conduct. This is far from the approach of those in the West, who may become preoccupied with rationally exploring ways of turning the negative sides of their character into positive qualities and at the end call it self-improvement. It is the belief in the East that what we are seeking *to be*, we already are, and it is the separation from our 'true nature' that produces the basic tensions of our lives.

Ritual purifications in many of the traditional martial and fine arts range from elaborate ceremonies involving flamboyant displays of purity performed by or on behalf of those involved to the delicate observance of simple, refined gestures. The purification of place and those in it brings a solemn dignity to proceedings and ensures that actions and thoughts are untainted. Karate may be modern by comparison with many of the traditional martial and fine arts, but they set examples which essentially carry right across all the Japanese arts. They all aim to ensure the environment is unsullied either by external influences or evil gods and to cleanse the participants of mundane cares or bad intentions and therefore to produce pure conditions from which pure actions unfold. What seems like almost fanatical observance of form and decorum is no more than getting directly to man's relentless spirit by cutting through all that clouds it.

For example, the preparatory formalities of the Japanese tea ceremony are rigidly planned to ensure that all signs of the guests' daily cares are removed before they enter the tea room. There is an initial period of silent reflection in a waiting lodge where all thoughts of the world outside dissolve in the contemplation of the peaceful surroundings and the guests commit themselves unreservedly to the world of silence. From here they are led by the host toward the tea house along single stones set a footstep apart. Their direction is fixed along a simple path; similar stones positioned across side paths form inviolable barriers. Before the tea house there will be a place where the actual purification of the guests takes place. It may be a flat stone with a hollow hewn out of its surface. A bamboo pipe channels fresh spring water into the hollow and the guests each take sips of the water from a simple bamboo scoop and let the water trickle over their hands. When this is done the symbolic ritual is complete and the guests are free to enter the world of tea and stillness.

It is worth elaborating here on the use of bamboo, whose symbolic significance cuts deep into Japanese thought. What equipment there is in the traditional arts of Japan often stresses the particular appeal of simple elegance and natural materials. The artistic craftsmanship involved in the process of refining raw bamboo for the Japanese bow or the *shakuhachi* (flute) is thought to endow the pieces with the unpretentious simplicity of the craftsman. The spirit of purity and stillness present during the process of making passes to the user, uniting with his spirit on his way toward his ultimate goal. Bamboo is thought to be an eternal symbol of the martial arts. It is seen as representing easy adaptability and, through its erect, graceful lines, it symbolizes upright, honest sincerity. It survives by yielding under the heaviest weight of snow, yet appears frail and brittle. While other inflexible branches give way under the strain, the bamboo offers no resistance, bending patiently until at an unforeseeable moment it lets the snow slip off, and it reasserts its long, upright form. The combination of a firm and solid exterior, harmoniously balanced with inner strength and plain simplicity, are the qualities best suited to man himself in the realization of his path toward his own 'natural centre'. The 'empty' meaning of *kara* in *karate* is symbolically represented by the empty centre of bamboo.

As a contrast to the delicate cleansing preliminaries of the tea ceremony, ritual purification of the place and the person reaches its most elaborate in sumo, the oldest of the martial arts. Enormous, near-naked men throwing clouds of salt and stamping extravagantly on a raised clay platform may appear almost ludicrous if the serious observance of such rituals was seen to be no more than mannerism or the eccentric prelude to combat. The ceremonial purification in sumo dates back to the seventeenth century. First the actual place is cleansed of all evil influences which may otherwise bear on the conduct of participants or discredit the proceedings. Ritual invitations are made to attract the god of creation — lucky charms such as dried chestnuts and cuttlefish are placed in an earthenware pot and buried in the centre of the ring while Shinto priests supervise. The wrestlers themselves before arriving at the tournament sprinkle handfuls of salt over their feet, so they start out clean. And at the ring-entering ceremony they clap their hands to attract sympathetic gods and stamp their feet (*shiko*) to frighten away evil spirits, raising their arms to show they are not concealing weapons. Lyall Watson has described the pre-match rituals:

> After entering the ring, the wrestlers throw salt (to purify the proceedings); warm up with one or two *shiko* stamps (to drive away any stray devils); squat; clap (to attract the attention of the gods); turn their palms up (to show they are unarmed); wipe their bodies with

tissues (for further purification); rinse their mouths with water (more ritual cleansing); spit with phenomenal accuracy into a pail; throw a bit more salt, perhaps licking some off their fingers (to sharpen the senses); and then crouch down on their marks and glare at each other.

Sumo wrestler performing a *shiko* stamp.

In a pure environment, then, combat takes place between those who have purified their thoughts and their bodies and declared their intentions to be honourable. All actions which ensue are then the product of such conditions.

Purity of place in all the arts reveals itself also in the

free use of simple, often natural, materials. Woven bamboo buckets of salt are placed in the corners of sumo rings and cedar buckets of water are used for the purification rituals. Every simple utensil at a tea ceremony has a rigidly prescribed purpose in the performance of the ceremony as well as the outward show of highly-developed artistic taste. In traditional karate *dojos* the wooden floor will be enthusiastically scrubbed and cleaned by the juniors to ensure it is uncontaminated. In all the arts there is a distinct absence of cumbersome gadgetry and extravagant forms. And so a karate *dojo* should be a simple, uncomplicated environment, for the same reason that traditional Japanese rooms and gardens are free from distracting features or decorative trimmings. Students ideally bring to an open space nothing but themselves. Whatever place we use as a *dojo* in the West and whatever clutter is left around by other users it is still, while we are there, our *dojo*, our 'place of the Way'. As the *dojo* should be free of distracting reminders of the outside world, so the students also should no longer be attached to outward things. In the same way that no outdoor shoes, or any other reminders of the outside world, are allowed on to a *dojo* floor, no everyday thoughts or daily cares should be present in the hearts or minds of the students. An appreciation of simplicity and an untroubled state of mind should be expressed in the initial bow of the students upon entering.

Whatever we do or whatever we make will be endowed with purity only if we are pure and inwardly content ourselves. And so the maker of a Japanese sword or bow or the craftsman of simple utensils used in the tea ceremony will endow the pieces with his own inner harmony which is then transmitted to the user. Likewise, a single brush stroke, a simple arrangement of flowers, the uncomplicated tilting of a fan in a dance or drama, or a martial art *kata* will be pure only if it derives from a pure, untroubled source. It shows itself also in such things as food, for which the Japanese have a reputation more for meticulous and decorative presentation than actual substance. If food is prepared under harmonious conditions and presented with simple refinement it will pass on to the consumer spiritual as well as bodily nourishment. The veneration of old or deceased masters in the martial arts is a recognition by young students that something of their spirit and inner virtues has been passed on to them.

The spirit of master swordsmiths in Japan was thought to have a quite remarkable influence on the outcome of the finished product, which was believed to hold within it the inspiration of the maker. In ceremonial dress, the maker would first invoke the blessing of his guardian god and prepare his sacred platform in accordance with traditional rites to purify his place of work. Consecrated ropes were laid around the workshop to keep away evil spirits and the master performed rituals of ablution to encourage and welcome his guardian god. When forging the iron bar and folding and refolding the blade and giving it baths of fire and water the master and his helper were in a highly intensified state of mind. The swords produced by masters were thought to be truly works of art of which something of divinity had entered. The sword is completed by a small round peg of bamboo passed through the handle to secure the blade in position, thus adding a small but functional symbol of nature which had been alive and grew in accordance with natural laws. The master swordsmith, Masamune, and one of his ablest disciples, Muramasa, were thought to transmit opposing qualities into their swords. There was something terrible about a Muramasa, yet something morally inspiring and humane about a Masamune. A legend tells of how someone tested the sharpness of swords made by each of these masters. He first placed a Muramasa blade in a current of water and saw that dead leaves floating downstream were sliced neatly in two. He then placed a Masamune blade in the same place and was alarmed to see how leaves floated around the blade avoiding its edge. The Muramasa blade was thought to be highly effective, but could not go beyond actually killing and there was nothing divinely inspiring about it, whereas the Masamune blade had absorbed from its maker the real ethical code for a *samurai*, which was to be a spiritual man, who uses his sword as a means of self-knowledge, rather than an agent of brutality who uses his sword as an instrument of death.

The true *samurai* was one who practised 'winning without fighting' rather than the one who fought regularly, however hard and well, for if all the qualities of a *samurai* were present there would be no necessity to fight. One well-known example of this tells of a master swordsman, Tsukehara Bokuden (1490-1572), journeying by boat on Lake Biwa. On being challenged by an aggressive and intemperate young *samurai* he replied that his art consisted of neither defeating nor being defeated, but conquering without drawing his sword. The young *samurai* persisted in his challenge, so Bokuden suggested they should settle the matter on a small island to avoid causing a disturbance on the boat. When the boat drew close to the island the hot-headed *samurai* jumped ashore and prepared to fight. Bokuden gave his sword to the oarsman and taking the oar pushed the boat back on to the lake leaving the young *samurai* stranded. 'That is victory without the sword,' Bokuden shouted to the marooned young *samurai*.

ETIQUETTE

As an expression of humility karate students bow slightly from the waist with heels together and hands at their sides when entering and leaving a *dojo*. All personal possessions have been left behind and there are no external signs of the outside world visible — no jewellery, no make-up, no nail varnish, ribbon or hair-oil. Apart from anything else it is a gesture of willingness to learn, perhaps even a moment of reflection at the boundary separating daily cares from personal, inner commitment. Ideally, to emphasize the separation, one should be entering a world of silence, where one's thoughts are turned inward, as the learning of any of the Japanese arts is an almost wordless process

devoid of fussiness or clamour. Those who arrive after the class has started should kneel at the entrance and, upon being beckoned to join the class, bow in their kneeling position and take their place.

Before and after practising with a partner a standing bow is performed by both students. Again, it is a slight bow from the waist, not a deep, extravagant gesture of servility or a perfunctory nod of the head. A 'safe' distance is maintained between the students, as the bow should be performed with the sense that a partner from this point on ceases to be anything but a potential enemy. For this reason the eyes remain at all times facing forward and all extraneous thoughts should be banished from the mind. The stature or grade of the partner should not influence the depth or sincerity of the bow. It is at once a mark of respect for the partner and for the movements to be performed, but it also lends an evenness to one's practice, as there should be no urgency and anticipation beforehand and no lingering grudges afterwards. The bow, therefore, is far more than a mere sporting gesture like boxers touching gloves before the final round of the contest or tennis players holding up new tennis balls to the opponent.

Before the lesson begins the whole class kneels and bows to the teacher, who returns what is a mark of respect and an action uniting all in a common purpose. At the end of a lesson, after a short period of silent meditation (*moksu*), the teacher and the class again exchange bows, this time adding a bow to the front of the hall where in traditional *dojos* there may be a small wooden shrine or scroll. (In the case of the Japan Karate Association *dojo* there is a picture of Funakoshi Gichin, the founder of modern-day karate, alongside the shrine. He appears to look down sternly on the performance and conduct of those he has influenced. The Japanese do not easily relinquish their memories or marks of respectful acknowledgment towards those who have made a significant contribution to their arts. In much the same way that the spirit of a master craftsman is passed on through his work to the user, the spirit and strength of elderly and past martial arts masters is thought to transfer to the hearts and minds of their students.)

In addition to these formalities, in traditional classes, or those in Britain which remain loyal to the proprieties shown in Japan, there will be a united reciting of the '*dojo* code', which reminds all present of their responsibilities towards themselves and to all around them. These words of loyalty, respect, sincerity will be called out one by one for the whole class to repeat and to take with them back into the daily workings of their lives. To the beginner they may seem at first like commandments, for they have similar ethical overtones. It is inevitable that this will be the case, as the English conveys only the raw meaning of the words, without the rhythmical power of the original Japanese.

- *Dojo kun!*
  Dojo code!
- *Hitotsu! Jinkaku kansei ni tsutomuru koto!*
  One! Exert oneself in the perfection of character!

- *Hitotsu! Makoto no michi o mamoru koto!*
  One! Be faithful and sincere!
- *Hitotsu! Doryoku no seishin o yashinau koto!*
  One! Cultivate the spirit of perseverance!
- *Hitotsu! Reigi o omonzuru koto!*
  One! Respect propriety!
- *Hitotsu! Kekki no yu o imashimuru koto!*
  One! Refrain from impetuous and violent behaviour!

Whatever technical advances we make during a lesson, the very last detail we encounter is therefore a resolution to take back into the outside world the spirit resounding from the words of the *dojo* code. We consciously empty ourselves of daily concerns before entering the controlled, simple space for training and we leave it behind carrying with us the spirit of the *dojo* code detailing in an uncomplicated way a code of ethics which we transmit to the world outside. It is, again, with the same degree of continuity that the craftsman of simple, natural artefacts passes on to the user the calm and unruffled spirit present during the making process. It is a measure of our stature just how much we are prepared to put our experiences in the *dojo* to use outside the formal place of training. For karate and the other martial arts have developed since their early days, when the emphasis was fully on the individual whose exclusive and ultimate goal was self-cultivation rather than contributing anything to the immediate environment or to society generally; students now properly extend their practice beyond the confines of the training *dojo*.

It is noteworthy, here, to mention that the Japanese value effort above technical ability, not least because technique can be merely a display of outer form while effort is more likely to penetrate inwards and as a result project outwardly a sincere and benevolent attitude to others. The more experienced we become at karate the more essential it is to maintain a sincere and undemonstrative attitude to those outside. As karate can be a ruthless instrument of violence if in the hands of those who abuse it, and as karate can attract to itself a suspicious reputation among those on the fringe, students must think of themselves as protecting its image and upholding its ideals at all times through their personal behaviour.

Observers of karate may feel that the ritualistic forms of etiquette within the actual process of training make up a large part of the external features of a karate session. In fact genuine karate has very little in the way of excessive ceremonial formalities, limiting its observances for moments where students by a simple gesture of a bow state to each other and their surroundings an absence of bad intentions. Although such conventions are strictly observed in all the disciplines and martials arts influenced by Zen, they do not form an impediment to what is the essential nature of the activity. There will be some students who attempt to conceal a lack of technical ability by embracing the formal rituals of bowing with uncontrolled enthusiasm, but as a general rule the simple, formal marks of respect form no obstruction between the student and his or her personal development. Each student in the *dojo* will be pursuing the same goal, and it is a mark of this that every student and teacher will adhere to exactly the same forms of etiquette. With this in mind it is necessary for Westerners to suppress any desire within a *dojo* to exhibit their own individuality as regards etiquette, which for some may represent a threat to personal values and a restraint of independent creativity. The realization of genuine aesthetic quality and artistic control, which are the fruits of constant practice, are more the result of being openly receptive than grafting new ideas on to existing personal idiosyncrasies.

As with many of the activities which come out of Japan there is in karate quite a rigidly followed heirarchical system among students. Older, more experienced or more advanced students (*sempai*, seniors) are responsible, to a large extent, for preserving *dojo* etiquette and elevating the spirit and conduct of the juniors (*kohai*). There is no abuse of power, no intimidation, but often a willingness on the part of *kohai* to earn their right in every respect to be in time *sempai* themselves. It will always be one of the seniors who will call out the *dojo* code for all to repeat, and in a Japanese *dojo* every lesson resounds with the constant shouts of *sempai* urging the class on when spirit wavers.

EQUIPMENT

Gi

Any loose-fitting sports clothes can be worn during the initial few weeks of training. Most teachers will allow this, but most beginners when they come to the point where they realize their involvement in karate is not going to be a brief affair will want to buy a proper *gi* (uniform). Apart from any other reason, beginners are more noticeable if they are not wearing the same outfit as everyone else in the class.

It is likely that most large sports shops now sell karate *gis*. But it is far better not to put your trust in a general salesman when it comes to buying what is the most fundamental piece of your equipment. There are now quite a number of specialist martial arts shops and suppliers, which will stock a range of *gis* and belts (*obi*) and you should get something resembling expert advice. Other students in your class will be able to advise you, or one of the many martial arts magazines will have advertisements placed by specialist shops, although this way you may need to buy by mail order, which is far from ideal. Some *dojos* have arrangements for buying *gis* in some quantity especially for new members, but by far the best approach is to go personally to a specialist shop.

A good quality *gi* should last up to three or four years, as long as you don't grow out of it. In any case, and this seems odd, avoid buying a *gi* that looks like it fits; it should when new look slightly too big. This is not because they shrink, but because the initial stiffness of a *gi* gives them a bulkiness which deceives the eye, making them look bigger than they are. The unnatural stiffness of a karate *gi* lasts no more than a couple of classes or the first wash, although they will usually feel slightly starched after washing, however old they are.

For a good *gi* you can pay up to £50 or £60, but this is for the best. If you really are sure that karate is for you, it is far better to make the investment and buy the best type from the start, which is a brand called *Tokaido*. There was a time when an unscrupulous British company was producing inferior *gis*, sewing *Tokaido* labels on, and passing them off as the original brand. It seems that authentic *Tokaido gis* are not now as rare in Britain as they were, so it should not be too difficult to buy the real thing. To be certain, ensure that both the top and bottom bear the *Tokaido* brand labels, that it feels very stiff, is very white in colour rather than a pale cream and that it is sold in its polythene bag also bearing the *Tokaido* symbol. (For young, fast-growing children, of course, *Tokaido gis* may not be worth the investment, in which case whichever type of *gi* is bought make sure that the fabric feels substantial, to the point that it feels almost intolerably stiff. Whatever you do, do not buy a judo *gi* as a cheaper or more easily available alternative. They are much heavier, designed to be tugged around, and the overall shape is different.)

The ties at the sides of the 'jacket' can either be used as intended or removed altogether. (As far as I know there are no *gis* specially designed for women, so a T-shirt of some sort needs to be worn underneath as *gis* often flap open at the front.) As a general rule avoid washing the *gi* too often in a washing machine, as it knocks the stuffing out of it. Apart from this, *gis* are white as a symbol of purity and the personal appreciation of this symbolic value is better expressed if the *gi* is washed frequently by hand rather than committing it to a washing machine and tumble drier. For the same reason, students should resist covering the *gi* with elaborate badges or embroidery.

Belt

A belt (*obi*) can be bought from any sports shop. The only consideration here is the length. The brand or quality makes no real difference at first; only the quality of the black belt matters, as this is the one that will last (at least in substance, if not in colour) as long as the student. Buy a belt that is too long rather than too short, as they have a habit of undoing themselves when new and inflexible, although if they are far too long certain movements cause the belt to flick the wearer in the face. Some people dye their belt the new colour as they advance in grade, but this in time leaves an unsightly rainbow colour around the waist of the *gi*.

Makiwara

Most of the training that students encounter involves techniques performed against an imaginary opponent or, when they practise with a partner, he or she is an opponent in feeling but not in reality, as all techniques are strictly controlled. Much of a student's time, therefore, is spent striking at air, which offers no resistance and is no test of whether the muscles are tensed correctly or whether the body's position would stand firm against an opposing force.

The *makiwara* (punching board) has never really been regarded as an essential piece of equipment in Britain, although in Japan it is thought of as indispensable. Before sparring techniques were introduced into training systems in the 1930s, karate students only practised the *katas* combined with intense practice on the *makiwara*. Techniques performed exclusively in empty, unresisting air were thought to lack real power unless the feeling for the techniques was consolidated by regular practice on an actual target. Apart from being an ideal way to learn distancing, the *makiwara*'s value lies in concentrating the power of the whole body at the precise moment of impact combined with an outrush of breath. Regular practice on a *makiwara* strengthens the parts of the body used in attacking or blocking, toughening the skin and knuckles.

The wood from which the board is made is either Japanese cypress or Japanese elder, which both have the required elasticity. Rice straw, or alternatively rubber and

Gyaku-zuki (reverse punch) to a *makiwara.*

Mae-geri (front kick).

heavy sponge wrapped with canvas, is used to cover the
part of the board that is actually hit.

An excellent brief account of how a *makiwara* should be
used is given in M. Nakayama's *Best Karate*, volume 1.
Unfortunately, though, most *dojos* in Britain do not
possess a *makiwara* and, where they do, few students take
it seriously. Certainly, no time within a lesson would be set
aside for *makiwara* practice. Students should not,
however, feel that their training is shallow if a *makiwara* is
not available to them, although regular training with one
adds an additional and exhilarating dimension to the
body's feeling which striking at empty air cannot supply.
They are very tricky to use at first, revealing very clearly
to a student an array of basic faults and inadequacies
which can otherwise go undetected for very long periods.

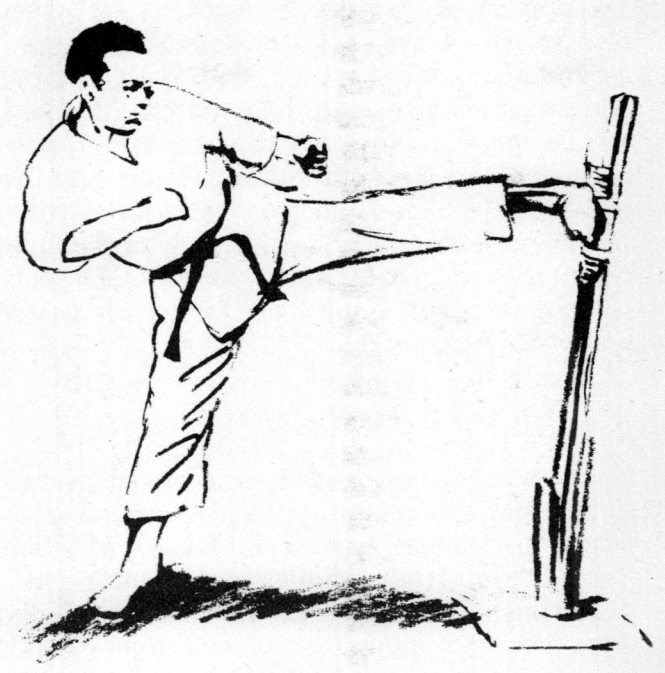

Yoko-geri kekomi (side thrust kick).

For example, any slight deviation from a straight line will cause the hand to glance past the striking pad, undermining the security of the stance; when the muscles tense at the wrong moment the hand will quite literally bounce off or cause the energy to vibrate back into the body rather than project outward from it. But those who persist soon appreciate a *makiwara*'s value in directing power through the body into and beyond a small area by coordinating all the parts of the body at a single moment.

A *makiwara* can be bought from martial arts shops, but it is far more satisfying to make your own. Depending on the type, they either bolt to a wall, or, preferably, are sunk into the ground. They are ideal to practise with at home, in the garden or garage, as they take up such a small amount of space. Students spend so much of their time practising

81

with others at a *dojo* that rarely are the benefits of solitary practice appreciated. In isolated silence, all that is heard is one's own breath. Nobody else can see successes or failures, and humiliations are personal. With a *makiwara* the critical moment is revealed by a thump of the pad as the breath catches and the body tenses. The *makiwara* is a passive, stationary object but it draws out the spirit from students who have relentlessly to concentrate the mind on the point just beyond that of impact. A dynamic rhythm can be built up and, apart from the physical advantages, students can find a satisfying peace from working alone at an actual unforgiving target.

THE TEACHER

The Japanese character for *sen* means 'ahead' or 'before'; the character for *sei* means 'life', 'birth', 'raw'. Together as *sensei* the translation, a poor one, is revealed as 'teacher', but it more appropriately signifies 'one who has gone before you spiritually in life'. It is used generally in Japan to address those to whom great respect is due.

A karate teacher's responsibility is huge. He does not normally seek out students, they come to him freely and commit themselves to his judgment. Under ideal circumstances students submit themselves unconditionally to a teacher's guidance, for a karate teacher is a particular kind of guide rather than an instructor, a mere purveyor of technical skills. The essence of karate cannot be laid out before students but reveals itself naturally to them in time, so it is not so much taught by a teacher but learned or absorbed by the students. What a good teacher first concentrates on is technique; hardly a word is needed about its significance, for students discover this for themselves and should be confident that they will. In many ways a student's own innate ability is responsible for progress. Teachers only assign students those tasks which they are capable of mastering; through constant practice, and therefore bodily sensitivity, students experience things for themselves. The teacher's role becomes more that of a passive onlooker than an active coach, as a student should not be swamped with technical nuances or overburdened with spiritual detail. The time comes when students need to be moved on to other tasks, and then the teacher steps in. Combined with imitation and repetition this still largely remains the foundation of all the traditional Ways in Japanese sports and arts.

The typical traditional method of Japanese tuition is for there to be quite uncomplicated directions with a minimal amount of theoretical instruction. Teachers should rarely speak but provide precise demonstration of the movements and techniques, without discussing or analysing them. Japanese terminology is used in all *dojos* for the movements, stances and for counting, but by associating words with actions Western students have no problem in quickly understanding what is meant.

In Britain most teachers are British, as there is only a handful of Japanese instructors. A large body of opinion is still more in favour of British teachers than Japanese, as they are thought to be more fully aware of Western students' needs and to be more sympathetic to their problems and technical deficiencies. Some people point to the possible limited knowledge of the English language of Japanese instructors. Karate, though, as we have seen above, is taught by demonstration not by lengthy, or even brief, explanations; this is based on the notion that one comes more completely and naturally to grips with technique and one's true spiritual objective through constant practice rather than the hit and miss circuitous route through the intellect. M. Nakayama, during a conversation about the principles and aims of karate, talked of how Japanese methods of tuition were adapted to accommodate the needs of American students.

In 1951, the Strategic Air Command sent 23 physical training instructors to the Kodokan in Tokyo to study the various martial arts under the leading instructors in Japan. This programme continued for 15 years, and it exposed a large number of Americans to correct principles of karate, judo, aikido and the other martial arts . . . In retrospect, I think the biggest impact resulting from our association with the Americans was that we were forced to find ways to explain karate to non-Japanese people. It immediately became apparent to me and to Master Funakoshi that if we were going to teach Americans, we would have to find a theoretical basis for our art. The Americans simply were not satisfied with following blindly like the Japanese. So, under Master Funakoshi's guidance, I began an intense study of kinetics, physiology, anatomy and hygienics. We believed that with a thorough grounding in the scientific basis of the body mechanics, we would find it easier to teach foreigners.

There are movements and stances in karate that have been handed down through the years and whose genesis sprang from such diverse sources as ancient horseman, peasant farmers, tranquil monks and so on. Some of the movements in the *katas* express such things as a student's affinity with nature. British instructors may see these as mere physical movements with a modern, practical application, or they may swamp the students with the historical context. Ultimately, though, it is not where the movements came from but where the students are going to that matters. Theory and technique are not the essence of karate, and teachers should avoid emphasizing them to the extent that students become little more than skilled puppets full of knowledge and vigour but empty of inner inspiration.

Japanese instructors have such a depth of understanding of the basics, the building blocks of the whole system, that infinite avenues of approach are constantly opened up to students. They are also, implicitly, to be trusted. Students submit nothing less than their entire welfare to the teacher and in return, and quite correctly, should feel that it is in good hands. To some this is like surrendering their freedom, for they are required to follow the teacher's guidance unconditionally along channels that are new to them. But in the same way that students are free to come, they are also free to go.

'TEACHING'

The principles of imitation and repetition in the Japanese arts underline the premise that the analytical faculties of the intellect are not of prime importance. Students imitate movements with no reference to critical appraisal of their worth or application. Little by little the actions are internalized, to the point where they manifest themselves from the students' own centre and the meaning of the actions is then conceived, in time, by the students themselves. However, along the way they should avoid mistaking technique for essence; the teacher's instruction is only regarded as 'the finger pointing at the moon, not the moon itself'. Like any other kind of guide, all a karate teacher does is point the way, then watch as people travel towards it. Diversions down side paths slow the journey down and suggest a conflict in the minds of those guided by the directions.

Unlike Western forms of repetitive drills, Japanese arts are based on the repetition of physical movements intended to cut through the tensions and encumbrances of the student's outer self and release an inner intuitive spontaneity. The aim is to make movements and techniques 'happen' automatically and without intention. The mind should be utterly unconscious of the action. A Japanese Zen master, Okada Torajiro, has described the benefits of repetition:

Keep a carp in a pond with a stone in the centre and another of equal size with nothing in the centre. In the pond where the stone is the carp swims round the stone all the time and thus has its exercise without meeting resistance. He grows more quickly than the carp in the other pond. This is the result of endless repetition.

A true 'master' of an action is one whose success is achieved not only occasionally or by chance but with absolute certainty. The repetitive process must penetrate the outer layer of moods and emotions to release the truly creative inspiration within. Most important, the resulting action must be sensitive to the least deviation, for it is not the eyes but the inner mind that first catches up a movement to which a response is needed.

Many sports and activities demand constant practice through repetition, with or without recourse to a person's analytical processes of thought. A musician practises his or her repertoire repeatedly until the physical movements concerned cannot possibly be performed wrongly, as this would involve the voice or fingers quite dramatically straying from the way in which they have been 'grooved'; at cricket schools a bowling machine can be set up to bowl a ball repeatedly to pitch on the same spot at the same speed and with the same amount of swing, so that the batsman can repeat the correct movement time and time again until he does it without thinking. The purpose is first to make the person respond consciously in the correct way and to make any necessary technical adjustments, but ultimately to reach the point where the gap between thought and response is non-existent. These approaches do have benefits as far as physical response is concerned, but it has to go deeper than that, for if a person becomes master only of physical techniques and not of themselves in changing circumstances the repetitions are little more than uncreative automatic drills.

A karate teacher of skill will occasionally conduct a lesson in a way that will take students to the very edge of exhaustion, and then slowly bring them back from it. There will be a large gap between what students believe they can reach and what they can actually reach. It is the teacher's responsibility to move the students' conception of their limits onwards to new boundaries, but to be aware at all times of the damage that can be caused if he or she continues to a truly unrealistic level. Apart from anything else it is a violation of the students' trust. Equally, inadequate training will always keep students within the bounds of what they are confident they can achieve, thereby never moving them on in their ability. The teacher should be aware of what the students are and what they can become. (It is unfortunately the case in some *dojos* that the teacher will quite deliberately not push students too hard for fear that he might be the only one present at his next class.) The resilience and persistence of students is not to be underrated, but the point of excessive physical effort should be clear and the motives of the teacher must appear genuine.

A karate lesson has fixed boundaries. Students can feel psychologically consoled by knowing that, say, at 8 o'clock they will start and after an hour they will stop. During that time they might be committed to non-stop practice of basics (*kihon*), combinations of techniques (*kata*) and various types of sparring with a partner (*kumite*). There is something psychologically unnerving for the students in not knowing how hard the lesson will be or how many repetitions of the movements they will be asked to perform. The temptation is for them to make adjustments to conserve energy in case the lesson is difficult technically or makes demands on their stamina which they think will be beyond them. (Ideally a *dojo* should not have a clock to prevent students 'pacing' themselves in this way.) It is this unpredictability which gives the repetition of karate movements unique value, for a tension exists between trying to perform every movement with full power as though it were the last and the feeling that the body's ability to continue is being eroded by exhaustion. Technique after a while begins to break down and the spirit takes over to prop it up. In the end the students are not even aware of what it is that moves them on. Clearly when this stage of training is reached the mind is redundant. After studying karate for some time it becomes apparent, through these periods of being taken to the point of exhaustion, that however much the body's ability to retain good form is reduced, the spirit does not dissolve but instead asserts itself ever more energetically. Students who have trained in this way will, in normal circumstances, always be functioning within an area they have already fully explored.

EXERCISES

Karate relies on speed and suppleness, particularly of the hips. Bulky muscles are more a hindrance than a help; although they may be strong, they will usually be slow. The muscles of a cat would be more suitable than those of a bulldog. To improve suppleness, lessons will always begin and often end with a series of exercises, usually working from the head down to the toes, but concentrating on improving the mobility of the hips. The area around the hips, particularly the stomach, is the most important area in all the Eastern arts; the stomach is where the feeling of strength and power derive and to where the breath is pushed. For the karate student, suppleness of the body represents strength. Ordinarily there are no weights or man-made machines used to promote strength or suppleness, and many of the exercises may seem similar to those used in an aerobic or yoga class.

Women starting karate should have no fear about developing heavy muscles, but they may see instead an increased definition in their existing body lines. Karate does nothing but improve the shape of the body and no area is deliberately hardened to form natural weapons, unless the *makiwara* is used excessively. Women are more

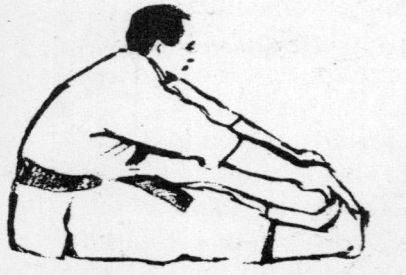

naturally supple around the hips than men, which gives them a distinct advantage. The natural shape of women makes them more flexible in that area, while the activities they may have pursued when young, such as dancing and gymnastics, would have loosened the joints at an early age.

WOMEN

A karate *dojo* may seem to be a predominantly male domain, so women may at first feel that they are gate-crashing or feel anxious about how easily and completely they will be accepted. Women are usually very clear and open, however, about their motives for starting karate, whereas men often suppress their motives or hide behind masculine pride. It is very rare to find even the slightest hint of discrimination or innuendo directed at any sincere student, either male or female, and it is probably unknown for women to be insincere either in their motives or their intentions.

Karate clubs often have a mix of men and women, boys and girls, all, for most of the time, performing on their own in empty space. Sometimes two people practise together, but this is not as often as people imagine, or perhaps as often as some would like. Karate, though, even when practised in pairs, does not become a contact sport —

women should not worry that they will be tugging, tripping and grappling on the floor as in judo. Karate respects the dignity and naturalness of the upright position — it is very rare for a karate student not to be on the soles of one or both feet. Women (and men) should not feel at a disadvantage by having avoided the rough and tumble of contact sports at school, for it is more the sports that have stretched the joints rather than jarred them that are an advantage.

A 'SPORT' FOR ALL

All *dojos* cater for all people. Any student who enters a *dojo* will be accepted. There are, of course, exceptions: as the truly aggressive or violent, unless they show a willingness to change, will find a karate *dojo* a very uncomfortable place to be; lazy students will not be debarred, but will find that they get little attention. Often, *dojos* will include students who have disabilities; those who have lost an arm or who are deaf, for instance, can easily make small adjustments and fit in entirely with regular lessons. (A black belt in Sensei Eneoda's *dojo* in the late 1960s was paralysed from the waist upwards. Special *katas* just using the feet and changes of stance were worked out, and his technique, because the upper part of the body was not in any way involved, was truly remarkable.)

GRADES AND GRADINGS

Karate grades and grading systems vary quite considerably according to the style of karate and the association. There are now numerous styles in Britain, and organizations which run them, although by far the largest is the *Shotokan* style administered by the Karate Union of Great Britain (KUGB).

Before students can start grading they are usually required to join the ruling organization of their style. They will then be supplied with a grading card or booklet in which their progress through the grades will be recorded. Gradings can usually be taken at three-monthly intervals, assuming that students have practised regularly.

Students will always start with a white belt and usually work through a series of colours, *kyu* grades, to the grades of black belt, *dan* grades. The advance through the *kyu* grades is seen as a maturing towards a solid foundation of technique, which is then built on in the *dan* grades. Real practice is thought to take place as one progresses through the black belt grades — *shodan* (the first black-belt grade) means 'first step', indicating that the *kyu* grades are technical preliminaries.

It is usual for the belt to get progressively darker as a student advances through the *kyu* grades, although this symbolic feature is now less clear through the introduction in Britain of orange and red coloured belts at the very early stages of training. A typical sequence of grades may be as follows:

kyu
9th	white
8th	white
7th	yellow
6th	green
5th	purple
4th	purple
3rd	brown
2nd	brown
1st	brown
1st *dan*	black belt
2nd *dan*	

Grading sessions are usually conducted by visiting instructors of sufficiently high grade. Sometimes a single club is involved, but members of several different clubs will often group together. They can be quite chaotic occasions, as students are usually on their mettle and tense. Most gradings follow a training session or are conducted at the end of a weekend or special course. Some students are unnerved by knowing their movements are being examined, while others find it exhilarating.

Grading sessions all follow a very simple formula. The grading instructor sits at a table, in front of which students perform *kihon*, *kata* and *kumite*. The lower grades are always called first and will be completely finished and free to watch when the higher grades are called. Students are called in small groups, usually four or six at a time. As their names are called each student stands, bows, and takes up his or her position to perform basic movements. Afterwards they return to their place, after bowing once again to the instructor. This will usually be repeated twice, to perform the *kata* and *kumite*.

PART 4
BASIC
PRINCIPLES

CONTROL

In the course of karate training students go to a *dojo* regularly to be taught an art of self-defence using the arms and legs systematically, so that any surprise attack can be controlled by a demonstration of strength equal to that of using actual weapons; they perform for years an infinite number of repetitions of techniques specifically designed to harm others if put to use; when they have come to terms with the techniques, and even along the way to this point, they are warned not even to think of applying the techniques in earnest outside the *dojo*. Students, then, dedicate themselves willingly and knowingly to an art which is built around practical usefulness, but they are in the end denied all use of its practical sides. It is a unique kind of control, amounting to a kind of restraint of trade, which reveals itself in other martial arts as well as karate. Japanese archers now spend their lives shooting arrows at a wooden or straw target (*mato*), and only ever at a target; swordsmanship (*kendo*) is practised with wooden imitation swords (*boken*) or bamboo sticks (*shinai*) only in a *dojo* with an imaginary opponent or one specially armoured.

It was not, of course, always the case. The traditional martial arts were originally effective and efficient systems of death until they came under the influence of Zen. The objects of attention were then reversed back on to the archer or swordsman himself and the system became the means through which, in a controlled setting, he overcame himself not an actual enemy on the field of battle. However erratic its development, karate now finds itself in the same position — it is a potentially lethal system practised by those who are themselves the targets of all their efforts. In a controlled setting people maintain total control over techniques designed to do extreme physical harm to others. Control, therefore, now divides into two distinct elements: control of the person; and the control of the techniques.

Control of the person
Personal control is that of a student who is dedicated to mastering technique, in full awareness that it will not be put to actual use. This injunction towards general self-control is embraced by the term *Karate ni sente nashi*, which is the inscription of Funakoshi Gichin's memorial. It has nothing to do with technique, but instead binds the student of karate to a strict code of behaviour. *Karate ni sente nashi* literally means that there is no first attack; it is broadly taken as a declaration on behalf of the student to maintain a defensive not an offensive spirit in all he or

she does. The karate *katas* reflect this, as the first movement is always defensive. Some go further still, starting with a movement expressing the student's affinity with nature. The first movement in the advanced *kata Kanku-dai*, for instance, is a slow raising of the hands with the forefingers and thumbs lightly touching at the tips and the palms facing outwards. The eyes look straight ahead until the hands reach the level of the eyes, when they follow the hands upwards to contemplate the sky through the triangular 'window' formed by the fingers. The *kata*'s name, *Kanku* comes from the first movements, 'looking at the sky'.

The first movement of *Kanku-dai*.

Karate ni sente nashi has a direct bearing on the conduct of modern-day karate students, but even in the more traditional martial arts actual fighting came to be an offence against Taoist principles. And pure Zen, following Taoism, demanded that weapons should only be used as a means to self-knowledge rather than instruments of murder. It was the fighter who remained alive without having released his arrow or drawn his sword that counted as the true Zen warrior — but, of course, he had also to retain his honour. His intention was to defeat without argument or conflict. So, again, we see that original Zen principles have filtered through into the fabric of the less-traditional martial arts such as karate. What is said today about the martial arts would not be radically different from what would have been said during those far-off days when Zen became the guiding influence. Thus, what has come down through the ages penetrates into the everyday existence of modern-day karate students. A Zen anecdote, once again concerning the master swordsman Bokuden (see page 71), illustrates the principle in the traditional martial arts of using a weapon only in case of extreme emergency.

The master, Bokuden, had three sons who were all trained in swordsmanship. To investigate their proficiency in the art of the sword he placed a cushion above a door curtain in such a way that it would be dislodged by anyone who entered. Bokuden called his eldest son. Even before entering the room the son noticed the cushion, so he took it down and placed it where it had originally been. Bokuden once again placed the cushion above the door curtain and called his second son. When the son entered he dislodged the cushion, but he caught it neatly and without fuss and replaced it. It was the third son's turn to enter. Full of confidence he entered and dislodged the cushion, but before it hit the floor he cut it in two with his sword. Bokuden then passed judgment on his sons. To the eldest he presented a beautiful sword declaring him to be well-qualified in his art and worthy of carrying a sword. He recommended that his second son should train even more assiduously. But the third son was pronounced to be a disgrace to his family and should never be allowed to carry a sword.

In the West gentleness and politeness can often be misunderstood as weakness. So any behaviour that is knowingly going to attract such accusations demands great fortitude to maintain. But this is what karate students are asked to do, even though they are better placed than most to exhibit their strength. The more one advances through the grades, the easier it becomes — in a sense one becomes bigger than the accusations. During the early stages, when some degree of technical ability has been reached, it is more difficult to achieve. There is a tendency to think of oneself as a kind of vigilante, protecting yourself and others against all and sundry whose bark is no more than a sign of personal insecurity, or even putting oneself in a position where a physical challenge is to be expected.

Sensei Nakayama has outlined the principle of *Karate ni sente nashi* as it applies to the modern-day karate student.

> *Karate ni sente nashi* is a strict prohibition against carelessly using the techniques of karate . . . A *karateka* should never act in a manner which could create an atmosphere of trouble, and he should avoid places where trouble is likely to occur. If a student frequents a bar where fights regularly occur and he is suddenly called upon to use his techniques in self-defence, then he does not understand the meaning of *Karate ni sente nashi*. In effect *he* started the fight because he knew trouble was likely, and he could have avoided the conflict altogether by simply not going there. *Karate ni sente nashi* is a wish for harmony among people . . . The *karateka* who understands this will have a modest heart, a gentle attitude and a wish for harmony.

Control of techniques

Control of techniques involves reconciling the power of an attack with the ability to stop it. The essence of all karate techniques is *kime*, the explosive power of an attack towards a target performed in the shortest possible time. The control of such a technique, stopping it just before the point of impact (reckoned to be about three centimetres), involves *sun-dome*. *Sun-dome* assumes *kime*; that is, there is no real beneficial control without real, absolute power. As karate involves striking with various parts of the body with maximum speed and power, while moving in different directions and maintaining balance and centre of gravity, control can easily be lost. But the combination of power and the ability to control it is what karate students in their training try constantly to achieve. The grading for the first black belt tests whether they have been successful. The instructor holds a pen or similar object in front of the student, and moves it constantly forward and backward and from side to side. The student aims a succession of punches at the pen with full power and total control, stopping just short of contact and varying distance and direction according to the pen's position.

Students who are best able to control their techniques are thought best able to control themselves. So the two elements of control are interlinked. Some people who are truly gentle to begin with still turn to a martial art. Others find gentleness and control through the discipline and freedom of hard training. And it is true control and real gentleness, rather than repression of a violent nature that remains below the surface and can yet break through. C.W. Nicol, in his book *Moving Zen: Karate as a Way to Gentleness*, tells of how he acted as an assailant against Sensei Nakayama for photographs appearing in a book on self-defence techniques.

> The Sensei got violently seized by the collar, by the throat, by the crotch. We went for him with clubs, sticks, broken bottles, razors, knives. He handled it all with such precise and focussed action that none of us ever got hurt. He hardly ever ruffled his hair or clothes, and yet I knew that the difference between living and dying under one of his focussed blows lay only in his mind.
>
> We held many sessions, and it was a lot of hard work, but I learned a lot about self-defence — it was as good as private lessons from the Chief Instructor.
>
> But that was not all I learned. One day, when we were

waiting at Yotsuya subway station, the train pulled in and a labourer barged out, crashing in to Nakayama Sensei. The man was a few feet away from me, but I tensed. He cursed the karate teacher, and had it been I, I would have shown him who he could and could not shove around. But Nakayama Sensei bowed very slightly and apologized, showing not even the slightest annoyance. The man went off, still muttering, and we all stepped on to the train.

Shotokan is a 'hard' style of karate in that the foot or hand usually moves the greatest possible distance from its starting position, when it is relaxed, to the end position, the target, when it is fully but momentarily tensed. The hands and feet, the usual weapons of a karate student, are the body's extremities. When they are extended at speed towards a target, the stomach (*hara*), which is the most important part of a karate student's body and thought to be its centre, is almost the sole cause of the technique's control or loss of it. The stomach is used to root the student to the ground, and when the base is strong the extremities are more easily controlled.

HARA

Karate students of whatever calibre are exhorted time and again during the course of training to use their stomachs. It seems odd to non-Japanese ears, but it is a clear instruction for students to lower the feeling they have for their bodies to the region called the *hara*, which for the Japanese represents the centre and source of physical and spiritual energy. Literally it means 'belly' or 'stomach', and is thought of as a reservoir from which all physical strength and performance is drawn and an 'ocean of energy' from which all spiritual well-being flows.

The *hara* implies to the Japanese nothing less than all that is essential for a person's physical constitution as well as their character, thinking and ultimate destiny. It penetrates so thoroughly into the culture and

consciousness that literally all human activity is measured by its presence or absence. When a person loses contact with it their whole physical world is turned upside down and their spiritual harmony is thrown into disarray.

Hara is not, however, a gift or privilege unique to the Orient; everybody is originally endowed with it. It is the duty of all to discover or, more correctly, rediscover this 'inner life force' when such things as emotions, intellect, wilfulness pull them away. This is achieved by obeying the laws of one's own nature, which means being physically and psychologically balanced in body and mind between the opposing poles of one's existence. As *hara* is the centre between the upper and lower parts of the body, man himself is centred between heaven and earth. He is physically rooted to earth but spiritually drawn towards heaven. This unity of three elements is symbolically represented by the form of a pagoda, where three tiers or layers represent earth, man and heaven. But this unity is, perhaps, most consciously preserved in Japanese flower arranging. A single branch with three stems symbolizes earth (*gyo*) at the bottom, often close to small rocks or a pool of water in the vase, heaven (*shin*, which also means 'spirit') which is a stem reaching upward, and man (*so*) between the two.

For the Japanese the bond with *hara* is revealed in outward behaviour, however trivial or grand, which displays not only the link with the determining physical centre of their being, but emphasizes *hara*'s importance to the complete or whole person. The way of walking, sitting, standing or even talking can show whether a feeling for *hara* is present. The Japanese aspire, metaphorically,

A single pine branch showing the three main lines of earth (*gyo*), man (*so*) and heaven (*shin*).

more to the shape of a sumo wrestler than an American
football player, whose triangular, top-heavy shape would
befit a man with *hara* only if turned upside down.

Representations of the Buddha, whether sitting or
standing upright with hands raised, show a pronounced
pot-belly. We can see the same emphasis in pictures of
Bodhisattvas, those who are able to reach *nirvana* or
enlightenment, and Kwannon, the Goddess of Mercy. And
in the many illustrations of Bodhidharma, the monk who,
as legend tells us, travelled from India to China and
instructed novices in rudimentary self-defence, the same
stress is seen around the region of the stomach. We in the
West, however, consider as bad form any sign of portliness
below the waist and good form anything that gives the
impression of stature emanating from the shoulders and
chest. Crossing one's legs, too, which in the West is
regarded as either a sign of modesty, self-containment or
simply composed comfort, is thought by the Japanese to
throw the feeling of *hara* out of line.

The Japanese language is infused with references to
hara, demonstrating quite literally all facets of a person's
make-up and personality, ranging from the voice to
benevolent behaviour and artistic sensibilities. There is no
generic equivalent in the English language which has such
a wide range of physical and psychological connotations as
the use of *hara* in Japanese. *Hara no aru hito*, for instance,
implies a magnanimous, spirited and even audacious
person who is never buffeted or flustered by the disruptive
influences of life. We talk about having a big heart: the
Japanese talk about having a big *hara*. Art, as we have
seen, is thought of in the East less in terms of a tangible,
finished object than what goes into the 'artist'. It matters
little if the 'artist' is a monk, karate master, woodcutter or
roofer, so long as the actual process of *doing* an activity
penetrates beyond the superficial layers of the ego and has
a beneficial effect on the inner person. Perfection,
therefore, in any art is only achieved by those conscious of
hara, which is expressed by the word *haragei*, literally
'belly art'. All the 'Ways' (*dos*) are characterized by

haragei — *shodo* (the Way of calligraphy), *chado* (the Way of tea), *bushido* or *budo* (the Way of the warrior, which includes the martial arts) as well as such everyday matters as personal relationships and conversing. *Harakiri* (*seppuku* for the *samurai*), the well-known term for ritual suicide by disembowelment, is essentially spilling life's essence, concentrating the incision on the very 'seat of life'.

The karate student's belt, when tied, separates the upper and lower body, and the knot, when pulled down slightly as it should be at the front, rests on a line with the *tanden*, a point within the *hara* about two inches below the navel. When the muscles of the abdomen are tensed correctly the focus of concentration and strength collects at this point, and it is where all the muscular impulses originate. We cannot cough, speak, breath or move without tensing the *tanden* muscles. It may be symbolically significant that in karate the colours of the belt get successively darker as the student advances through the grades — a mark of recognition that the student is becoming better able to activate the *tanden* by gathering the strength from all the parts of the body and concentrating it at the point where the knot of the belt rests. In the same way, sumo wrestlers are presented with sumptuously embroidered aprons, called *kesho-mawashi*, by wealthy and knowledgeable patrons. These are worn around the stomach at the pre-match parade before the audience as a show of rank and experience. The Grand Champion is allowed to wear the snow-white hawser, called a *tsuna*, which can weigh up to 32 lb and symbolizes his status and authority. In stark contrast to this the West shows its appreciation of status and rank by adorning the upper part of the body, particularly the shoulders and chest, with medals, stripes and fancy epaulettes, which give a pronounced squareness to the shape of the body. Different styles of headwear in the West can also be a sign of military rank or position, whereas in sumo, for instance, a referee, if demoted to the lower ranks, is made to wear different footwear denoting a fall in status.

Sumo wrestler in hawser (*tsuna*) and ceremonial apron
(*kesho-mawashi*).

Breathing with the abdomen ensures that the energies
concentrated in the *tanden* are spread evenly upwards and
downwards throughout the body. This, in effect, means
the whole body is breathing, thus ensuring that the upper
and lower parts of the body retain their natural unity. In
practical terms for the karate student this is vitally
important, for the lower body must form a stable base with
the ground while allowing complete mobility of the upper
body. The lower body must grip the earth through the
energies released from the *hara*, as though drawing
sustenance from it, in the same way that a tree grows and
flourishes by extracting life from its root system. It is only
through the proper use of the stomach that a firm stance
can be achieved, as though the feet were glued to the
ground, not consciously but by the energies flowing from
the stomach. The feet play no active part in the process,
although many students consciously grip with the toes,
which only serves to lift part of the feet off the ground,

thereby reducing the surface area of contact, and causing unwanted tension in the ankles. Any part of the body becomes tense if one deliberately puts one's consciousness into it.

The *hara* can not only be thought of as a sort of central control room from which energies are evenly distributed upwards and downwards, but also the decisive element in the support and balance of the whole body. The shoulders are the main cause of loss of balance, for they are the most mobile part of the trunk. In general, the more relaxed the shoulders the more relaxed the whole body. Yet it is the shoulders which give way to tension most readily. They involuntarily jerk up when the person is surprised and become tight and hunched-up when nervous or anxious. The strength from the *tanden* should be such that it acts as if the upper part of the body did not exist at all. In the upright position man should feel strength in the *tanden* as though his body had grown perpendicularly straight up from the centre of the earth.

Every physical object has a centre of gravity, that point about which the weight is evenly balanced in any position. As soon as man gets to his feet his centre of gravity comes into evidence. The dogged insistence in the West that strength and energy are most prominent in the upper body expresses a harmful tendency away from the natural centre of gravity of the human body. And when the centre of gravity of any object is disturbed, the tendency is for it to lose balance or topple over altogether. The centre of gravity of man is the *tanden*; if prominence is given to any other part of the body he will easily be pushed over or unbalanced.

Gravitational pull dominates all things. Man has to resist this force to maintain his natural upright position, or be dominated by it. When man is standing upright gravitational force falls in a plumb-line from the crown of the head, through the body and trunk, emerging between the legs. If the *tanden* is misplaced it emerges through the heels and the body will submit to the force and be drawn downwards. Such is man's predicament. Originally designed to walk on four legs he now stays on two only by exercising his autonomous will upon a constant downward pull.

Kiba-dachi (straddle-leg or horse riding stance).

KIAI AND BREATHING

It is well known to most people that karate students 'shout' when they perform techniques. It is probably thought they do so to put fear into the opponent. This shout in karate is called *kiai*, made up of *ki* (energy, spirit, mind) and *ai* (union, coming together), so the actual noise made by the shout is not the whole point of the exercise; rather the shout is the product of the *kiai*, the 'coming together of energy'. It is not a long animal-like scream as portrayed in films, but a short moment of extreme focus expressed vocally.

A *kiai* is performed at pre-set moments, usually two, during *katas*, and relatively freely during basic training and when practising with a partner. It is performed at the very end of a movement as the muscles tense and the breath is caught.

Only about 80 per cent of the breath is exhaled at any time, as the body is at its slowest and is most vulnerable after exhalation and when breathing in. A complete exhalation of breath leaves the body limp and unable to respond quickly to the next movement. All physical exertion is performed when the breath is being exhaled, as the ease with which a heavy object can be lifted when breathing out, compared to breathing in, will show. We cannot speak, either, when breathing in, or, for that matter, when holding our breath. It is the exhalation of breath, then, that is vital and which is the point of departure of all movement.

As in all the martial arts and Zen disciplines, breathing is in principle abdominal; it relies on the diaphragm. The more air we take in, the more blood will be supplied to the lungs and heart. Shallow breathing, therefore, can easily lead to fatigue and tension; and it is unnatural, despite it having become almost second nature to many people. We should breath fully and from the depths of the body, from the diaphragm rather than the larynx, and it is from deep inside that the *kiai* emerges.

MUSHIN

The white belt that all beginners wear in karate represents purity or innocence. At this early stage of training the student has a sense of unconfined freedom, which he can give full rein to, unhindered by thoughts of technique or self-consciousness. If attacked he responds naturally; not, perhaps, with much elegance or with any recourse to technique, but with spontaneity and innocence. If applied to sport in general he would be in the position of having 'beginner's luck', which is nothing more than being oblivious to the intricacies of the game or the correct method of playing it — he often succeeds through sheer effrontery because he throws himself in at the deep end with irrepressible abandon.

As the student of karate advances through the grades he learns a technical system of defence and devises clever strategies and complex manoeuvres. His innocence abandons him, along with his self-confidence, as he can no longer act as freely and spontaneously. He becomes aware of all the possible ways that the techniques he himself is learning could be used against him. Essentially he is worse off than he was before, as he is now forced to admit that he is at the mercy of all others whose strength and technique is greater than his. What he now knows and practises is something of a burden, as his mind fixes on specific movements and techniques which previously he had no awareness of.

As he passes through the *kyu* grades to the degrees of black belt his technique becomes refined and established. The black cotton which covers the tough canvas of his belt begins to fade with perpetual use, and the whiteness beneath begins to show through. After many years his technique 'happens' intuitively and he no longer fixes his mind on specific movements but has heightened awareness of all his surroundings. He returns, then, once again to his state of freedom and innocence he had at the beginning, but it is now complemented with a rare knowledge and skill, which is completely divorced from conscious effort. His belt, through years of use, will have shed most of its black cotton outer layer and the white beneath will show through, completing the cycle.

This, essentially, is the principle behind *mushin* (*mu*, empty; *shin*, heart, mind, spirit), usually translated as 'no mind' or 'empty mind'. The mind should take in everything about it, which should be experienced but not dwelt on. This accords with the Zen principle that one should be attached to nothing in particular, for when the mind fixes on a specific object or movement it is 'stopped' and therefore excludes all else around it. *Mushin*, therefore, is not simply an intense form of concentration, which blocks out all external distractions, such as the state a person may be in when totally absorbed in reading a book or watching a film.

When practising with a partner in karate none of his or her movements should be the sole object of attention; the mind should be 'everywhere and nowhere', increasing the peripheral vision to take in the entire range of possibilities. This can be seen clearly in many sports. A batsman in cricket, even though 'looking' at the ball as he hits it, can time and time again place it one side or the other of a fielder who should at that moment be out of 'sight'; a squash player usually knows where the opponent is even though his attention is on the ball. D.T. Suzuki illustrates *mushin* by taking all the leaves on a tree as an example:

> When I look at a tree, I perceive one of the leaves is red, and my mind 'stops' with this leaf. When this happens, I see just one leaf and fail to take cognizance of the innumerable other leaves of the tree. If instead of this I look at the tree without any preconceived ideas, I shall see all the leaves. One leaf effectively 'stops' my mind from seeing all the rest. But when the mind moves on without 'stopping' it takes up hundreds of thousands of leaves without fail.

This, in practical terms, can be applied to a man opposed by many others. He can only achieve victory if, after he has disposed of one opponent, he does not dwell on it but allows his mind to go directly on to the next. This is very clearly demonstrated in the proper performance of the *katas*, which are in principle ritual battles against several imaginary opponents. Each movement flows into the next without any dwelling on past movements, whether good or bad, and without any anticipation of those to follow.

In *mushin* the mind is not distracted by intrusive thoughts, although such thoughts in karate, as well as in everyday life, are a constant temptation. Personal matters concerning the world outside can easily drift in and out of the mind; thoughts of what happened before the lesson or what one is going to do afterwards break the mind free of dealing exclusively with the present. The following Zen anecdote about the Zen master, Tanzan, and his disciple, Ekido, amusingly illustrates how past events can linger in the mind:

> Tanzan and Ekido were once travelling together in the heavy rain down a muddy road. Coming around a bend they met a lovely young girl in a beautiful silk kimono and sash who was unable to cross the muddy intersection. Tanzan offered to help and lifting her in his arms he carried her over the mud.
>
> They continued their journey, but Ekido did not speak again until that night when they reached a lodging temple. He could no longer restrain himself. 'We monks do not go near females,' he told Tanzan, 'especially not young and lovely girls. It is dangerous. Why did you do it?'
>
> 'I left the girl there,' Tanzan replied, coolly. 'Are you still carrying her?'

The thoughts most difficult to keep from following while training are those concerned with the technical intricacies of the movements themselves or those concerning the behaviour of the body. No matter how rarely or regularly a student practises their body will exhibit quite unfathomable varieties of 'moods'. Quite often students will blame on their body the faults of their mind, but equally often the body, for quite irrational reasons, does not respond as one expects. It is listless or lively for no apparent reason. Thoughts about how the body has responded previously can distract a student's attention from how it is responding at the present. A movement which a student was previously able to perform suddenly deserts them and they get engrossed in the technical reasons why this has happened; a stance which they found they could do comfortably now feels awkward or painful and they become involved in making slight adjustments; a mistake made in a movement of a *kata* may prey on the mind as the rest of the *kata* is completed. Conversely, students may become in some ways elated by the way their body is performing and so still be thinking of past success when performing other movements. Thoughts of future techniques may also come to mind. In a *kata* one particular movement may be thought of as a stumbling block, so all movements leading up to it may be clouded by anticipation or anxiety. *Katas* must finish in exactly the same place as they started, so students who feel themselves straying out of position can become absorbed in making adjustments to their stances so that the ending of the *kata* is at least in the correct position.

Practising on the *makiwara* (see page 78) gives a student clear indication of performance at the present moment. Any thoughts which might linger in the mind about past failures or successes in striking the board reflect badly on the student's present movements. A *makiwara* allows the student no flexibility of the mind — either he directs his mind absolutely on to the board and hits it, with the satisfying thud of success, or his mind wanders off and the target defeats him.

The idea of *mushin* is not an archaic concept confined only to activities with attachments to Zen and with no relevance today. It is one of the many areas of the martial arts that topple over easily into our everyday life. Although well disguised, it revealed itself in the Michael Cimino film *The Deer Hunter*. It is a film very much concerned with 'one shot', or one chance to survive, regulated by the power of the mind bearing on a physical object, in this case a bullet.

Michael, Steven and Nick, the three main characters in the film, are captured by the Vietcong. Michael and Nick are forced to play Russian roulette with a gun containing one bullet, while the Vietcong guards bet on who will win – that is, who will survive. Michael believes their only chance of escape is for him and Nick to play each other with three bullets in the gun and take the guards by surprise. His plan means that both he and Nick would at first have to play the game for real. He insists that they must both totally forget about rescuing Steven; they must both clear their minds completely of all external thoughts. Only with an empty mind fixed on the 'one shot' will they be able to 'will' an empty chamber in the gun.

KATA

Before sparring (*kumite*) was introduced in the 1930s *katas* were the soul of karate. Essentially they still are, but the presence of sparring has to some extent undermined their value in the minds of more competitive students. Every single basic movement that students perform as an individual technique was drawn from the *katas*. They are performed alone, no other students being involved, although occasionally they are practised in groups to give students a proper feeling for the techniques against 'real' opponents. Essentially they are ritual battles against several 'imagined' opponents who 'attack' the student from all sides with a variety of arm and leg movements as well as, on occasion, with sticks and poles. They are, then, highly practical, each movement representing an authentic attack or defence, the 'enemy' being seen with the mind's eye.

Each *kata* is self-contained. They start on one spot with a bow to the front. The *kata* is then performed and should finish on the same spot with another bow to the front. The two bows at the beginning and end are considered as part of the *kata*, not a topping and tailing with formal etiquette.

The first and last movements of the *katas* themselves are critical. The first movement is always defensive, and follows immediately after a moment of complete inactivity and composure called *kamae*, 'readiness'. Research into brain-wave patterns have revealed that karate students exhibit a calmness in *kamae* equal to yogis and Zen monks in meditation. The first defensive movement, then, is an explosion of energy from an absolute state of calm to its extreme opposite. The last movement is usually offensive — the student, in performing the *kata*, emerges victorious over others as well as over himself — and is held in *zanshin* (*zan*, to remain, to continue; *shin*, heart, mind, spirit), which can be thought of as the resonances in the student gradually fading away, like the dying away of a bow-string's vibrations or the slow death of a single note of music. Only then is the *kata* completed with the bow.

There are about fifty *katas* which have come down to the present day, but it is not necessary to know more than about sixteen until the very high black-belt grades. To get to the *shodan* grade one need only know seven — the five *heian katas, Tekki shodan* and *Bassai-dai* — but for completeness, the sixteen *katas* which are usually known by the *nidan* grade are given below.

Heian shodan	*Bassai-dai*
Heian nidan	*Kanku-dai*
Heian sandan	*Empi*
Heian yondan	*Hangetsu*
Heian godan	*Jitte*
Tekki shodan	*Gangaku*
Tekki nidan	*Jion*
Tekki sandan	*Nijushiho*

The origins of the karate *katas* are not known, but many of them contain individual characteristics which give some idea of how they may have developed. Some contain movements which are suggestive of the primitive hunter returning to camp after the kill, demonstrating by expressive ritualistic mime how he overcame his prey. Others have slow, flowing movements combined with vigorous bursts of speed and sudden changes of position, which Funakoshi Gichin believed had influenced Okinawan folk dances, or been influenced by them (see pages 15-16). Okinawan peasants, once denied the right to carry any kind of weapon, turned instead to their simple farming implements, while others practised, in secret, systems of self-defence using any part of the body which fitted the purpose. It could be assumed in these cases that any conflict would be against several opponents, so continuous and varied movements, such as those found in the *katas* of today, would have resulted.

The first movement of *Heian shodan*.

The first movement of *Heian nidan*.

The first movement of *Heian sandan* and *Heian godan*.

The first movement of *Heian yondan*.

The first movement of *Tekki shodan*.

Whatever the origins of the *katas*, it is during the performance of them today that students touch the warrior instincts of their ancestors. They serve as a dynamic, moving record of the past, continuing the line from itinerant monks, professional *samurai*, innocent peasants and the secretive élite to the irrepressible mastery of Funakoshi Gichin, who gave them shape and order and comprehensible names and passed them on to those who would take them into the modern age.

KIHON (BASICS)

Until the 1930s techniques in karate were only found within the context of the *katas*, but since then they have been practised in isolation, repeated over and over again. The belief is that the stronger the individual component of karate the stronger the whole system, in much the same way that a building is more sturdy if each individual brick is sound. But there is another reason, and so the ancient

Japanese term *ikken hissatsu* has reasserted itself and has become the fundamental practical motivation behind training methods — the meaning here is 'to stop an opponent with a single blow'.

The movements of karate are structured, precise and symmetrical and usually move in straight, uncomplicated lines. They bear no resemblance to the crude, undisciplined, but possibly effective, flailing, gouging, swinging and poking one would expect from an unarmed, untrained, but desperate person. This is not to say, however, that effectiveness in karate is in the least sacrificed to clean, structured technique and good form. An uncontrolled flurry is only sometimes effective yet always wastes energy (apart from having nothing to do with personal prowess or skill). A single punch, however, from a trained karate student can travel at a speed of thirteen metres a second and exert destructive force. So effectiveness can be realized within one thirteenth of a second or so, depending on distance — equivalent to the time it takes to sneeze or blow out a candle.

Every technique must be performed with *kime*, the concentration of power realized at the end of a movement and achieved by the explosion of energy from complete rest to its opposite extreme. This means, in effect, that a hand or foot propelled away from the body towards a target at great speed, needs to be suddenly and completely halted in its progress at the moment when the arm or leg straightens. If it is not, real *kime* will not exist and damage can be done to the knee or elbow. If we tied a weight to a length of string and, holding the free end, threw the weight away from us, the violent jerk of the string as it snaps straight at the moment the weight reaches its furthest point would represent the critical moment of *kime*. In karate the 'jerk' of the arm or leg during a punching or kicking technique is checked by momentary muscular tension, centrally controlled by the stomach, in particular the *tanden*.

The basic techniques in karate — punching (*tsuki*), kicking (*keri*), striking (*uchi*) and blocking (*uke*) — can be

Oi-zuki (lunge punch).

Mae-geri (front kick).

Yoko-geri kekomi (side thrust kick).

Ushiro-geri (basic kick).

Shuto-uke (knife-hand block).

Empi-uchi (elbow strike).

applied to various levels of *kumite* (sparring), practised within the *katas* themselves or built up into sometimes quite complex combinations and practised in their own right. All gradings involve basic techniques, simple or not so simple combinations (increasing in complexity with grade), a *kata* and sparring (which becomes freer and less predictable as grade increases).

KUMITE

It was not until the late 1920s that *kumite* came into prominence and, again, all techniques were extracted from the *katas*. Although *kumite* appears to be, at least visually, more in line with what most people imagine karate to represent, it is in fact, still in its infancy compared with the *katas*, although it often threatens to swamp the older, more-established set forms in many dojos.

Although every attack and every block can be practised with a partner, there is a fixed sequence of *kumite* structures that are used throughout the grading systems.

Kumite ranges from the very basic five-step or single-step, where the type of attack is known and the target area is announced, to the totally free kind of sparring, which is used in advanced gradings and in competition.

The body falls into three target areas — *jodan, chudan* and *gedan: jodan* covers the region from the neck upwards; *chudan* is from the waist to the neck; and *gedan* is below the waist. In basic *kumite* the target area, either *jodan, chudan* or *gedan*, is stated by the attacker, who then attacks with a single, straightforward technique, which is known by the opponent. The freer the type of *kumite* the less predictable the target area and the attacker can feint, manoeuvre for position and distance, and undermine the opponent's defences and therefore time the attack to his or her own advantage.

CONCLUSION

What, then, are the benefits of karate in a world in a hurry, which demands quick results and tramples on those who don't achieve any, at least any that are visible? It is easy to say that the qualities demanded of a karate student — determination, concentration, control, persistence, self-discipline, etc. — account for the success of Japanese industry and, if applied outside in the same manner as in the *dojo*, can improve or even transform our lives. The question to be answered seems more to be whether karate as a way ultimately to self-knowledge, can still lay claim to any relevance when the industrialized, businesslike world rushes about us. When the outside world pours its acclaim and financial support on to those whose physical achievements are visible it may seem perverse to turn one's attention, in some cases redirect one's whole life, into an art which aims at invisible inner harmony and turns its back on competing for medals and rewards.

A world free from conflict and rivalry can now scarcely be imagined. It is common to believe that the world has never been so violent, and difficult not to think of localized areas of conflict as symptoms of a general malaise. What, then, is the point of taking up a martial art, which gives every indication of improving our ability to protect ourselves in a hostile world, if its true purpose is actually weighted more dramatically towards improving personal spiritual growth? Where there are hostilities it may seem more reasonable to ensure survival by becoming even more physically hostile than more spiritually calm. For, in a dark alley, facing a knife glistening in a street lamp, is inner harmony a more potent weapon than a history of successful street fighting?

There is no escape from the anxieties that constant practice in karate induces. Its practical applications, if used effectively, are claimed to be capable of saving our lives. But the question which hovers constantly in our minds is that, at the moment of actual physical threat, will

it in fact 'work', or will we be reduced to a knotted bundle
of fear? On a spiritual level, will our training in karate
ensure that an unflagging spirit shines through at the most
demanding moments of our lives, when our physical
strength alone is not enough? If karate claims to be so
beneficial in terms of physical stature and control as well
as spiritual well-being, there may be the tendency to feel
that possessing such qualities is a form of alienation,
amounting to something like a tactical withdrawal from
the nuts and bolts of everyday life, leaving students
unable to fit in with the inadequate strengths and
everyday emotions of those around them.

If the general tone of what has been said before leans too
heavily towards the spiritual improvement of the person,
the balance here must be redressed, for all the martial arts
were originally developed for practical reasons — to
protect oneself or to destroy others. All students who now
practise these arts inherit, to a large extent, the instincts
of those who have gone before and who have contributed to
what comes down to us today. They may have been
religious monks wandering mountains riddled with
marauding bandits, or simple-minded peasants wielding
crude farming implements and swinging rice flails in a
stand against pillaging neighbours or intemperate
overlords. On the other hand they may have been
highly-trained warriors whose day-to-day trade was
killing, usually because it was their vocation to protect
their lords (*samurai* is derived from *saburau*, 'to serve', 'to
attend to') but sometimes just for the sake of idle
recreation. Although karate today is not, as some think, a
training ground of refined thuggery, its seeds still lie in the
kind of ruthless utilitarianism employed in the mountain
passes, on the Okinawan farms and on the fields of battle.
Even though the aims of the martial arts have now swung
round to point squarely at the person doing the arts,
nothing in terms of their effectiveness has changed. All the
actions of the karate student are performed with the same
intent as they ever were, even though opponents are now
always imagined. The lethal movements practised are not

a kind of incidental platform upon which we build spiritual maturity, or an excuse to perform a sort of dynamic aerobics which leads to all-round fitness. The belief that whatever is physical is also spiritual often applies equally if reversed. So, back in the dark alley, facing the knife glistening in the street lamp, the karate student's body automatically reacts in exactly the same way that it has done time and time again during training in the *dojo*.

It is perhaps significant that, with all its martial arts systems, kick boxing and wrestling gyms, with its *dojos* ringing to the sound of martial artists going through the practical motions of annihilating imaginary rivals, street fights and bar-room brawls are almost non-existent in Japan, and one can walk in safety, alone, at any time of the day or night in any Japanese city. It is as though the true spirit of the martial and traditional arts has penetrated deep into the fabric of everyday Japanese life.

PART 5 REFERENCE SECTION

GLOSSARY OF TERMS

Boken
Wooden practice sword used in *kendo*, which is close to the weight and feel of the real thing.

Budo
The martial arts. Literally 'the Way of combat'. The emphasis is on the character *do*, 'Way' or 'Path'.

Bujutsu
Preceded *budo* as the practical approach for warriors on the field of battle.

Bushido
'The Way of the warrior', the medieval code of the
samurai.

Chado
'The Way of tea'.

Chudan
Area of the body between the waist and neck.

Dan
Grade of black belt in karate, judo, etc. Literally 'step';
shodan, *nidan*, etc. mean 'first step', 'second step', and so
on.

Do
'Way' or 'Path' (to enlightenment).

Dojo
'The place of the Way'. Training hall for the martial arts
or Zen meditation. Place of awakening.

Gedan
Area of the body below the waist.

Gi
Karate or judo uniform.

Hakama
Version of the traditional Japanese kimono still worn for
kendo and archery.

Hara
Literally 'belly' or 'stomach', thought in the East to be a
person's 'vital centre' of physical energy and spiritual
well-being.

Haragei
'Belly art'. Thought to be every activity of a person made
perfect through *hara*. Perfect art.

Harakiri
Colloquial word for ritual suicide, 'to split the belly'.

Jodan
Area of the body from the neck up.

Judo
'The gentle way'; *ju* means 'pliable' or 'adaptable'.

Kado
'The Way of flowers'. The unity of three elements, earth, man, heaven are characterized by *gyo*, *so* and *shin*.

Kamae
'Readiness', state of claim alertness prior to movement.

Kanku dai
High-grade *kata* in karate, meaning 'looking at the sky'.

Karate
'Empty hand': *kara*, 'empty'; *te*, 'hand'. Originally meant 'Chinese hand' until Funakoshi Gichin proposed the change of the character for *kara* in 1935.

Karate ni sente nashi
Generally regarded as a statement for overall self-control, but literally means that there is no first attack in karate.

Kata
Pre-arranged forms against several imagined attackers. The five *heian* katas are the first to be taught in karate, followed by *Tekki shodan* and *Bassai-dai*.

Kendo
'The Way of the sword'.

Keri
Karate kicks.

Kesho-mawashi
Ceremonial apron worn by sumo wrestlers.

Kiai
Karate 'shout'. *Ki*, 'energy, spirit, mind'; *ai*, 'union, coming together'.

Kihon
'Basics'. *Kihon kata* is sometimes the first basic *kata* taught in karate.

Kime
Explosive power of a karate technique from complete rest to its opposite extreme. Literally 'finish'.

Kohai
Junior or lower grade.

Kumite
Sparring with a partner. *Gohon kumite*, five-step kumite; *kihon-ippon*, basic one-step kumite; *jyu-ippon*, one-step free sparring; *jyu-kumite*, free sparring.

Kung Fu
Chinese martial art. The more correct title is *Wu Shu*, but the name *Kung Fu* is now widely accepted.

Kyu
Coloured-belt grades ranging from ninth *kyu* to first *kyu*.

Kyudo
'The Way of the bow'. Japanese archery.

Makiwara
Practice punching board.

Mato
Target in *kyudo*.

Moksu
Period of silent 'meditation' at the end of a karate lesson.

Mushin
'No mind' or 'empty mind': *mu*, 'empty'; *shin*, 'heart, mind, spirit'. Where the mind does not 'fix' on a specific object or movement but takes in entire surroundings.

Samurai
Japanese warriors in feudal times. Derives from *saburau*, meaning 'to serve, to attend to'.

Sempai
Senior high-graded students in karate.

Sensei
Teacher: from *sen*, 'ahead, before' and *sei*, 'life, birth'. Literally 'those who have gone before'.

Shiko
Stamping in sumo to ward off evil spirits.

Shinai
Bamboo practice sword used in *kendo*.

Shizen-tai
Natural stance in karate.

Shodo
'The Way of writing'. Calligraphy.

Shotokan
Karate 'style' founded by Funakoshi Gichin. The word has no arcane meaning; *Shoto* was Funakoshi Gichin's pen name; *kan* means 'building'.

Sun-dome
Control of karate techniques just before contact with a target.

Tanden
A person's centre of gravity, within the *hara* about 2 inches below the navel. Centre from where all muscular impulses originate.

Tsuki
Karate punching techniques.

Tsuna
Hawser worn by Grand Champion in sumo during the ring entering ceremony and preliminary rituals.

Uchi
Karate striking techniques.

Uke
Karate blocking techniques.

Zanshin
An alert, unattached state of mind: *zan*, 'to remain, to continue'; *shin*, 'heart, mind, spirit'.

Zenkutsu-dachi
Front stance in karate.

FURTHER READING

The following list is of course by no means complete. It avoids the many colourful, how-to-be-a-champion books, on the assumption that pictures of authors putting their fists through bricks or posing in impressive fighting stances do nothing but isolate readers, or at best leave them cold. Instead, the list aims to supply a cross-section of reading covering many of the Japanese martial, traditional and fine arts, as they all have so much in common. In addition, there are more general books on Zen and Japanese culture and those covering the main concerns raised in the substance of this book. All books mentioned are available in bookshops at the time of writing.

Karate-do Kyohan, Gichin Funakoshi (Kodansha, Tokyo). First published in 1935, this was the first major book published on karate. It is here that Gichin Funakoshi, the founder of modern-day Japanese karate, proposed radical changes to many established principles, which at first caused such a furore among traditional Okinawan karate masters but which dragged karate from its secretive, elitist past and projected it into the modern age.

Karate-do: My Way of Life, Gichin Funakoshi (Kodansha, Tokyo, 1985).
A frank and absorbing autobiography from Gichin Funakoshi's early days in Okinawa to just before his death at the age of 88 in the 1950s. An intriguing picture of the author's lifetime involvement with karate through the years of Meiji to the establishment of the Japan Karate Association, it includes many amusing and revealing anecdotes about the author and the emergence of karate as a world art.

Best Karate, vols 1-9, Masatoshi Nakayama (Kodansha, Tokyo, 1987).
A step-by-step guide from very basic techniques to the

high-grade *katas* by the successor to Gichin Funakoshi as
Chief Instructor of the Japan Karate Association. It
includes numerous exceptional photographs of many
outstanding Japanese instructors, and so stands head and
shoulders above all other books on karate principles and
technique.

Conversations with the Master: Masatoshi Nakayama,
Randall G. Hassell (Focus Publications, St Louis, 1983).
A lengthy conversation between a journalist and Sensei
Nakayama, which covers the history and philosophy of
karate. What is revealed, here, is quite simply unique and
unavailable elsewhere.

Moving Zen: Karate as a Way to Gentleness, C.W. Nicol
(Paul H. Crompton, London 1985).
A moving, personal memoir of the author's two and a half
years in Japan, his progress from complete beginner to
black belt and how karate broke down his tough, violent
exterior to expose a gentle, tranquil nature beneath. A
perfect companion to serious books on technique and the
more solid philosophical treatises, it follows the day-to-day
struggles of a dedicated student looking for spiritual
meaning through intense physical training. One of the
most sensible and controlled books on karate written by a
foreigner.

Zen in the Art of Archery, Eugen Herrigel (Arkana,
London, 1953).
This small book has long been recognized as the
indispensable account of the relationship between Zen and
the art of archery. Unquestionably a classic in its field and
relevant to all studying a Japanese art. The final chapter
is an interpretation of *mushin,* taken from a famous letter
on swordsmanship.

Kyudo: The Art of Zen Archery, Hans Joachim Stein
(Element Books, Shaftesbury, 1988).
A thorough introduction to the Way of the bow.

Particularly useful as it discusses in depth the development of Japanese culture and its spiritual values as well as the introduction of Taoism and Zen Buddhism into Japan and how these influenced modern martial arts.

The Way of the Sword, Reinhard Kammer; *The Tengu-geijutsu-ron* of Chozan Shissai (Arkana, London, 1978).
A treatise on the relationship between Zen and swordsmanship. The introduction and interpretation by Reinhard Kammer pulls together the many strands of Shissai's thought, applying them more broadly across all other areas of life and other arts.

Sumo, Lyall Watson (Sidgwick & Jackson (Channel 4), London, 1988).
This highly-illustrated book captures in absorbing, slightly ironic tones the oldest martial art and the big men involved. In particular, the heirarchical structure of sumo and the meaning of the elaborate ritualistic ceremonies have direct relevance to the entire sphere of Japanese arts.

Zen in the Art of the Tea Ceremony, Horst Hammitzsch (Penguin, London, 1982).
The traditional Zen art of the tea ceremony, its grace, harmony and, in particular, its tranquillity, to which all the Ways ultimately lead, is described here in charming detail. It manages to strike a perfect balance between simplicity and depth.

Zen in the Art of Flower Arrangement, Gustie Herrigel (Arkana, London, 1958).
A delightful book which brings to life the significance and symbolism underlying this serious Zen art.

Zen and Japanese Culture, D.T. Suzuki (Princeton University Press, 1973).
This deals with the influence of Zen across the whole spectrum of the Japanese martial and fine arts and is

considered the indispensable classic of its kind. It includes the substance of the famous letter by Takuan, a Zen abbot, to the master swordsman, Yagyu-Munenori, which summarizes the concept of *mushin*.

The Zen Way to the Martial Arts, Taisen Deshimaru (Century Hutchinson, London, 1982).
Rather idiosyncratic, but at times illuminating, particularly in its appraisal of the martial arts as opposed to Western sports and attitudes.

Zen in the Martial Arts, Joe Hyams (Bantam, New York, 1982).
Sensational in parts, but interesting for the comparisons it makes between the spiritual side of the martial arts and one's everyday life.

The Chrysanthemum and the Sword, Ruth Benedict (Tuttle, Tokyo, 1972).
A thorough guide to Japanese culture and practical ethics and a valuable source of background information which has direct bearings on how the Japanese approach their arts.

Hara: The Vital Centre of Man, Karlfried Graf Dürckheim (Mandala/Unwin Hyman, London, 1962).
An evocative book which probes deeply into the reasons why man has become isolated from his environment, his spiritual well-being and his physical stability by losing touch with his 'vital centre'. A book that makes readers take a close examination of the way they conduct their lives, in particular those who are involved in the arts.

Homo Ludens: A Study of the Play Element in Culture, J. Huizinga (Routledge, London, 1980).
A serious and highly compelling study focusing on the connection between play and contest, which asks why people do activities which are at once 'pointless and significant'. A crucial study for all those involved in sport or competition.

USEFUL ADDRESSES

Great Britain
Karate Union of Great Britain
Maychalk House
8 Musters Road
West Bridgford
Nottingham NG2 7LP

Martial Arts Commission
First Floor
Broadway House
15/16 Deptford Broadway
London SE8 4PE

English Karate Council
Mr D. Mitchell
188-94 Old Street
London EC1

Scottish Karate Board of Control
Mr D. Bryceland
74 Lamington Road
Glasgow G52 2SE
Scotland

Welsh Karate Federation
Mr K. Mumberson
Smalldrink
Parsonage Lane
Begelly
Kilgetty
Dyfed

Northern Ireland Karate Board
Mr T. Boyle
52 Raby Street
Ormeau Road
Belfast 2
Northern Ireland

British Kung Fu Council
Mr M. Coley
Shao-Lynn
39 Tower Street
Kings Lynn
Norfolk

United British Taekwondo
Mr A. Marie
9 Shrub Court
18 Cedar Road
Sutton
Surrey

British Jiu Jitsu Association
Mr R. Clark
Barlows Lane
Fazakerley
Liverpool L9 9EH

British Shorinji Kempo Association
Mr R. Jarman
31 Fairlawn Grove
Chiswick
London W4

UK Tang Soo Do Federation
Mr M.K. Loke
44 Holden Way
Upminster
Essex RM14 1BT

UK Sul Ki Do Federation
Mr M.Y. Kim
First Floor
472 Caledonian Road
London N7 8TB

British Thai Boxing Board of Control
Mr Ryan
63 Carr Meadow
Willow Vale
Clayton Brook
Nr. Preston PR5 8HR

Nippon Dai Budo Kai
Ms B. Stewart
Barlows Lane
Fazakerley
Liverpool L9 9EH

British Student Karate-do Federation
140 Southend Arterial Road
Hornchurch
Essex RM2

United States
United States Karate Association
Mr J.K. Evans
PO Box 1500
Greenfield
CA 93927
USA

Canada
National Karate Association
Mr R. Tordiffe
45 Cambridge Street North
Lindsay
Ontario K9V 4C8
Canada

Australia
F.A.K.O.
Mr J. Newman
Suite 4
First Floor
122 Cambridge Street
Canley Heights
New South Wales 2166
Australia

New Zealand
New Zealand Karate Association
Mr P. Shepherd
10 Kenley Place
Avondale
Auckland 1207
New Zealand

INDEX

Page numbers in *italics* refer to illustrations